The technique of audio post-production in video and film

D1396039

The library of communication techniques

Film

The technique of editing 16 mm films
John Burder

The technique of film editing
Karel Reisz and Gavin Millar

The technique of the professional make-up artist for film, television and stage
Vincent J-R Kehoe

The technique of special effects cinematography
Raymond Fielding

Television

The technique of lighting for television and motion pictures
Gerald Millerson

The technique of special effects in television
Bernard Wilkie

The technique of television news
Ivor Yorke

The technique of television production
Gerald Millerson

Sound

The sound studio
Alec Nisbett

Radio production
Robert McLeish

The technique of audio post-production in video and film
Tim Amyes

The technique of audio post-production in video and film

Tim Amyes

Focal Press

Focal Press
An imprint of Butterworth-Heinemann Ltd
Linacre House, Jordan Hill, Oxford OX2 8DP

$\mathcal{R}$ A member of the Reed Elsevier plc group

OXFORD   LONDON   BOSTON
MUNICH   NEW DELHI   SINGAPORE   SYDNEY
TOKYO   TORONTO   WELLINGTON

First published 1990
Paperback edition 1993
Reprinted 1994

© Butterworth-Heinemann Ltd 1990

British Library Cataloguing in Publication Data
Amyes, Tim
   The technique of audio post-production in video and film.
   (The library of communication techniques)
   1. Cinematography. Sound recording and sound
   synchronization
   I. Title II. Series
   778.5344

ISBN 0 240 51363 0

Library of Congress Cataloguing in Publication Data
Amyes, Tim
   The technique of audio post-production in video and film/
   Tim Amyes
   p. cm.
   Includes index
   ISBN 0 240 51363 0
   1. Sound motion pictures 2. Sound – Recording and
   reproducing
   3. Video tapes – Editing 4. Motion pictures – Editing
   I. Title
   TR897.A44 1990
   778.5'2344—dc20   90-2236

Printed and bound in Great Britain by the University Press, Cambridge

Preface

As technology develops, audio post-production becomes more and more sophisticated and specialized. To grasp and understand all the aspects of the art becomes more and more difficult. New languages of technical jargon are developed which seem designed to confuse the uninitiated.

This book explains modern video and film audio post-production techniques, (the theory and practical applications) in simple understandable terms.

It is intended as a book for interested amateurs, audio students or professionals, who are looking for a complete understanding of the industry from location recording through to theatrical release or transmission.

Acknowledgements

The author wishes to express his gratitude to the following organizations and their staff for their help in providing information for the development of this book: in Britain – Amek, Anglia Television, BBC, Dolby Laboratories, FWO Bauch, Mag Masters, Mersey Television, Molinaire, Saunders and Gordon, Scottish Television and Siemens Neve in the USA – Editel, Lexicon, Magna Sound, Magnosound, New England Digital, Photomagnetic, the Universal Recording Corporation and the Chicago Caveat group.

In addition I should like to thank the Scottish Television Staff Trust for granting me a Research and Travel Scholarship.

The following companies have kindly provided drawings and diagrams; M. W. Albrecht, Audio Kinetics, Branch and Appleby, CMX, Digifex, DeWolfe, Dolby Labs, Eastman Kodak, JVC Professional, Klark Teknik, Lexicon Opus, Neve, Sony Broadcast and Studer Revox.

Dolby, Dolby Stereo and the double D symbol are trademarks of Dolby Laboratories Licensing Corporation.

Contents

An historical background

Since man first reproduced images on a screen he has wished to add sound to increase the illusion of reality. Thomas Edison's laboratory is credited with producing the world's first moving talking picture when Edison's assistant walked towards the Edison sound camera lifted his hat and said, 'Good morning Mr Edison'.

The pictures were viewed in a 'What the butler saw' device and the sound was heard through acoustic headphones. This was very much a personal viewing and listening system. There was no electrical amplification system and therefore no way of acoustically projecting the sound to an audience, and there was certainly no system to alter or improve the sound once it had been recorded. The techniques of audio post-production would not be perfected for another 30 years or more. However, in less than ten years the basic technology needed to successfully produce sound/motion pictures had been developed.

In 1904 Eugene Lauste, a Frenchman working in London, managed to successfully record sound onto a piece of photographic film. Now it was possible to record sound on the same piece of film as picture, and to copy it simply by printing it photographically onto another piece of film. Despite this technical breakthrough there was still no way to successfully amplify sound, although attempts were made to use compressed air systems, with some success. It was not until Lee de Forest invented the electronic amplifying valve or tube in 1914 that successful projection of both sound and picture to a large audience was possible.

In 1926 the world's first commercially successful sound feature film was made in America, 'The Jazz Singer', using cumbersome gramophone discs synchronized with pictures. The object was not to make a dialogue film, but to produce a film that would no longer require a live orchestra as a musical accompaniment – thereby producing a massive cost saving for the exhibitor. At the same time as these sound feature films were being made, Fox's 'Movietone News' was introduced, recording actual events as they were happening. Originally, each sound newsreel item was introduced with silent titles, but it was soon realized that commentaries and music could enliven the 'reels'. Therefore, methods were developed which would allow a commentary to be added with music. The techniques of audio post-production were being developed.

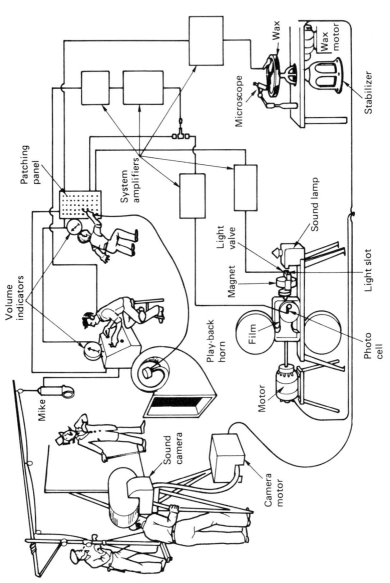

The Western Electric sound recording system of 1929 film and disc recording

Within the next fifteen years the film industry developed all the basic operational techniques needed to produce a polished quality soundtrack; techniques that are used today both in film and video productions; techniques that allow various separate soundtracks to be locked together in perfect synchronization, and then to be mixed together to produce a final completed soundtrack. Nothing is new. In the early 1930s Western Electric produced a photographic noise reduction process, anticipating Dolby. In 1939 stereo sound arrived in the cinema with the Walt Disney film Fantasia. Even today's multitrack music recording techniques were anticipated by Hollywood's large studios who used multiple track photographic sound recording systems in the 1930s.

The post-synchronization or replacement of dialogue with dialogue in another language was an early development. The Silent film's international market was lost with the introduction of the 'talkie' and America was particularly badly hit. The American product needed a larger market than just the English speaking world, so post-synchronization was developed, allowing dialogue to be re-recorded in a foreign language after a film had been edited and completed.

During the Second World War there were further developments in electronics that would affect the film industry; it became apparent that Germany had developed a new and revolutionary recording system, superior to disc or film. A system that explained how Hitler had managed to deliver speeches that were apparently live in places so far apart that he could not have had time to travel between them. The secret was magnetic recording. It was of a higher quality than even the best 'push-pull' photographic soundtracks available at the time. It was now no longer necessary to wait for photographic processing before playing back film recordings; sound could now be heard immediately. However, every move forward has a tendency to mark a step back. Sound editors complained that, with the new-fangled magnetic sound, it was no longer possible to see the actual optical sound modulation on the track. This tended to make sound editing more difficult. (Today, with audio post-production work stations using digital sound, this facility is once again available.)

In the early 1950s the film industry began to feel the competition of television and it responded by producing wide screen pictures, with stereophonic sound of the highest quality.

These early stereo feature films were produced in true stereo. The dialogue was recorded in stereo on the set. This meant that each time the picture cut, the dialogue moved its screen position – perhaps even in mid-sentence – as one picture was edited onto the next. This discontinuous stereo sound was unacceptable. It became standard practice to record sound in mono on location and to move it about the large sound field the cinema provides, in the audio post-production process.

Early stereo magnetic striped films had their problems too for they tended to shed oxide and clog projectors, muffling the sound (magnetic stereo release prints tend to be used nowadays only for special presentations and first runs) and cinema owners returned to showing poor quality monophonic optical soundtracks.

However, in the home the quality of sound reproduction was improving. The long playing record and the Hi-fi system had arrived, but perhaps,

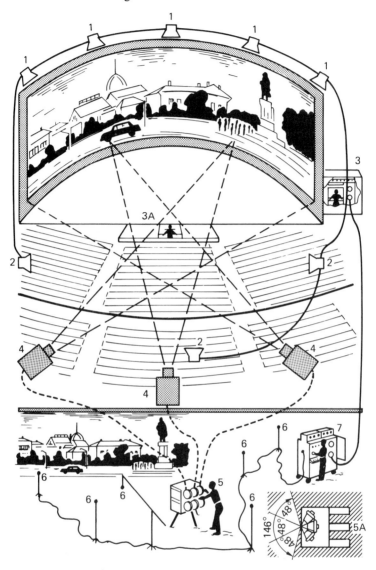

The Cinerama film; 1, rear screen loudspeakers; 2, ambient surround loudspeakers; 3, projection sound control; 4, three synchronized projectors; 5, camera 5A camera arrangement; 6, microphones for stereo sound; 7, sound mixing

because of lack of interest from the consumer the television set still sat in the corner of the room producing Lo-fi sound. Indeed, manufacturers had tried hard in the 1930s to increase television sales by offering quality wireless receivers capable not only of long and medium wave reception but also picking up VHF television sound. These efforts were unsuccessful, as were the attempts to offer full sound radio facilities on television receivers. By the late 1940s television sound transmission had been relegated to being the Cinderella of broadcasting. The total audio amplification part of a receiver was often just one valve, the pictures were small and the sound limited. Styling restrictions and the effects of stray magnetic fields from the loudspeaker on to the picture tube, all resulted in the use of small speakers and poor sound quality. This produced a situation which was not conducive to technical or aesthetic improvements.

Television was a live medium. It was quite unlike film, where events were recorded and painstakingly recreated; a television programme once transmitted was lost forever. In television there was no minute examination of detail and no post-production situation. A repeat was a second performance – a complete re-creation of a live programme. Like a theatrical production, the T.V. show either had to go on or just go off the air – a situation completely different from film making. In 1955 the situation began to change; the BBC went on the air in London with a recorded programme. The recording machine was called Vera (Video Electronic Recording Apparatus) and used a high tape speed of 200 inches/second (as opposed to the standard audio speed of 15 inches/ second) but the quality was poor. Two years later the world's first quality commercial videotape recorder was introduced by Ampex.

The Ampex videotape recorder produced pictures capable of a definition up to 4 million cycles per second. It was originally intended to allow live television programmes to be recorded on America's east coast, and then time-delayed for transmission at the 'same time' hours later, on the west coast. This system spawned two new techniques in television – editing and post-production. Originally, a razor blade was used to cut and edit videotape, but this was soon replaced by systems designed for editing by copying the pictures from one machine to another.

With the introduction of video picture editing it became apparent, as the film industry had discovered in 1927, that the sound track also needed editing and 'sweetening'. Since it was very expensive to tie-in film sound editing systems to videotape, another system was required – one which would be as flexible and versatile as film. The multitrack tape recorder from the music studio provided an answer. It could produce many different soundtracks all in synchronization and linked to the picture; and to achieve this a special electronic code was developed rather like the sprockets used in film – time code.

Today film and video post-production systems offer similar technical facilities, and a quality of reproduced sound that can be exceptional. Good quality sound reproduction is available from all but the smallest television sets and in the cinema it is possible to produce excellent sound quality despite difficult acoustic conditions.

In the mid 1980s digital audio recording became available to music studios and through compact discs to the general public at home. This is the ultimate in recording quality; a quality which is closely duplicated in the domestic video cassette recorder, now offered with a Hi-fi capability.

Audio post-production systems also offer digital recording. This is a particular'y appropriate system since sound is recorded on data disks where the perfect quality is matched by almost instant access. As technology progresses it will be possible for more and more material to be recorded onto these disks. Digital audio consoles, originally used in the

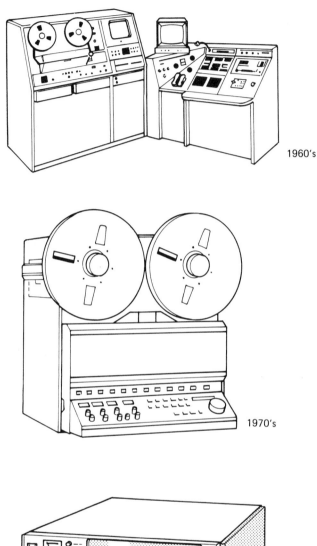

1960's

1970's

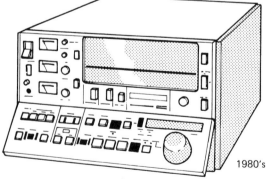

1980's

The shrinking size of videotape equipment has led to the introduction of video cameras and recorders comparable in size to film equipment, encouraging the development of sophisticated audio post-production equipment. The 1990s will see the introduction of small digital video recorders

record industry, have been developed for audio post-production too, where their ease of automation can be used to its fullest extent.

The technical aspects of audio post-production have changed dramatically over the years. However, the basic need is the same, namely to lay or build soundtracks, (the sounds that go with the pictures) and then to mix them creatively to produce a cohesive soundtrack to counterpoint and expand on the pictures.

In many discussions on sound reproduction the term 'quality' (i.e. technical perfection) seems to be applied as the only criteria for judging sound. However, discussions on visual reproduction use the term 'quality' as only a part of the overall judgement; for photography is often considered on artistic grounds as well as that of technical quality. Likewise, we ought to consider the soundtrack in terms of artistic judgements, for sound is part of the whole creative work.

In audio post-production it is important that the audio mixer has respect for both the pictures and the sound he controls, since there is an interaction between the two. The sound image and the vision must be cohesive; if they conflict the viewer will be lost.

The basic functions of the soundtrack are as follows:

1. To enhance the pictures and to point up visual effects.
2. To add three-dimensional perspective to the single-dimensional picture, even without stereo.
3. To enhance realism with sound effects and acoustics.
4. To give a geographical location to pictures that may be visually unrelated.
5. To add dramatic impact with music and effects, perhaps with counterpoint
6. To add contrast by changes in volume.
7. To provide programme sound that is intelligible and easy to listen to, in every listening condition.

2

Video, film and pictures

The purpose of this book is to describe audio post-production techniques. However, to fully understand the post-production process a basic knowledge of picture recording is necessary, and in this chapter we look at the basic technology behind video recording and photographic picture recording.

Moving images, whether they be stored on film or videotape, are nothing more than a series of stationary pictures, each slightly different from the previous one and each capturing a successive movement in time. When these pictures are shown or projected at speed, the brain interprets them as continuous motion, a phenomenon known as persistence of vision.

It takes approximately a 20th of a second or 50 ms (micro-seconds) to visually register a change in an image. When the images change at greater speeds than this, we see pictures that move.

Film

A film camera records pictures photographically. This is achieved by pulling down a ribbon of film using a claw which engages onto a sprocket and positions this emulsion stationary infront of the lens. A shutter operates for a fraction of a second to expose the image on the film and then, while the shutter is closed, the next frame of unexposed photographic film is positioned (pulled down) for the shutter to open again for exposure.

The image is reproduced in a projector and in order to reduce 'flicker' each image is reproduced twice. Three international width formats are used, 16 mm and 35 mm for television use, and 35 mm and 70 mm for cinema use.

The intermittent movement produced in a film camera is unsuitable for sound recording, which requires continuous smooth motion. Sound is therefore recorded either separately on an oxide coated audio film on another machine held in synchronization with the picture (double system) or, alternatively, the recording is made at a point away from the picture where the intermittent motion of the claw can be smoothed out (above the picture-head in 35 mm and below it in 16 mm). Film normally runs at a speed of 24 or 25 frames per second.

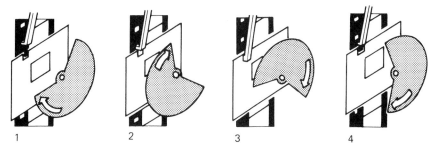

The claw and shutter mechanism of a film camera; 1, exposure of the film; 2, claw pull down; 3, film advanced; 4, shutter opens again (*From S. Bernstein, 1988, by permission*)

Video

The television system works on a similar principle to that of film using persistence of vision. However, the image is produced as an electrical waveform, so instead of focusing the image onto a photographic emulsion, the television camera focuses its image onto a photosensitive cell made up of many thousands of elements. These are scanned by an electronic beam which picks up the variations in light on the screen, and breaks the picture down into its separate elements. These are sent one after another, sequentially, to the transmitter or recorder.

To reproduce the picture, an electron beam which is 'controlled' by the camera is directed onto a phosphor screen that forms the front of the television monitor, tracing a picture. The beam is muted during its 'fly back' journey from the top to the bottom of the screen in order to stop spurious images being seen. The electron beam scans the picture at a speed of 15 625 times per second. Each vertical scan is called a 'field'. On the European Pal 625 line system, 25 complete pictures are presented every second and the screen is scanned 50 times. In America, on the NTSC system, 525 lines are produced at 30 frames per second with scanning taking place 60 times. Since the picture has been split up by scanning, it is important that it is reassembled in step with the camera. Two pulses are sent to ensure this, one a line scan pulse and one a field scan pulse.

Video recording

A colour video signal has a band width of 5.5 MHz and specialist techniques are needed to record this signal. A normal audio tape recorder is entirely unsuitable for this purpose, since it can only record a range of 10 octaves, whereas, to record video successfully an 18 octave range is required. On a normal tape machine, with a fixed longitudinal head, this would require speeds of many miles per hour. The only practical way of achieving this necessary speed is by using a rotating head, which scans the tape at a high speed, while the tape itself runs at a speed similar to an ordinary audio tape recorder. A special control track is recorded to

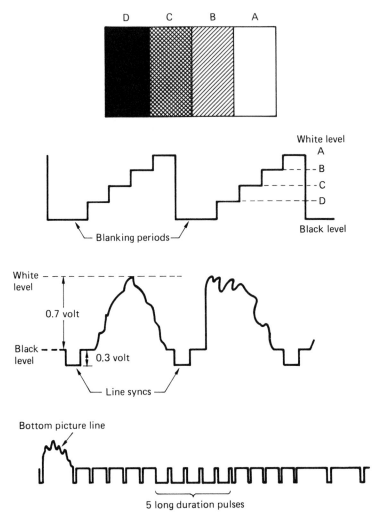

The conversion of a picture to a television signal. The picture ABCD is converted into various signal voltages. In the blanking period between the lines the electron beam flies back, the sync pulses are added at the end of each field to keep the camera and receiver in step (*Courtesy of Robinson and Beard*)

precisely define the position of the recording drum on the tape. This allows the head to be positioned correctly to replay the recorded picture.

The scanning head was first successfully used by Ampex in 1956, when it launched its 2 inch quadruplex video recorder. In this format, four heads are equally spaced around the edge of the spinning head drum. This is mounted at right angles to the tape, one head taking over the recording when the previous head leaves the tape. Stationary images cannot be viewed on this format. The linear speed is 15 inches per second but the effective recording speed is over 100 ft per second.

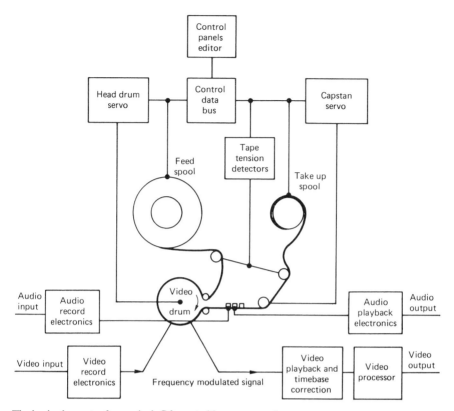

The basic elements of a one-inch C format videotape recorder

One inch format

The 2 inch format is no longer in general use. It was replaced in the late 1970s by the 1 inch format. In 'C' form, which is used in Britain and the USA, the tape is 1 inch wide and wrapped around the head drum in the form of a helix. The head rotates in nearly the same plane as the tape and records video tracks which are at an angle of only 2.5 degrees to the edge of the tape. This makes it possible to stop the tape to view a still frame, and by moving the tape slowly, viewing in slow motion is possible.

With the 1 inch format only one recording head is used. This means that there is a small gap called the 'format drop-out', where there is no picture information when the head leaves contact with the tape. This gap is arranged in the field blanking and on replay, additional information is provided from reference pulses. Some American broadcasters requested information to be provided for the whole of the field and the original 'C' format has an additional recording head mounted 33 degrees in advance of the main head. This was not included in EBU European machines, and this has meant that a fourth audio track is available.

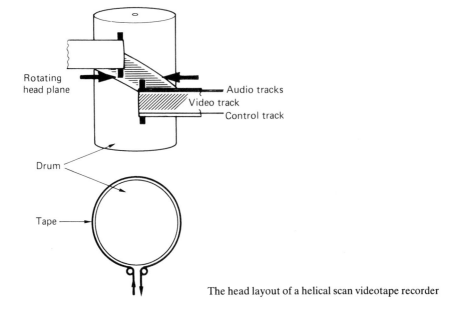

Rotating head plane

Audio tracks

Video track

Control track

Drum

Tape

The head layout of a helical scan videotape recorder

Video cassette recorders

In the 1970s videotape began to replace film in the broadcasting industry. A small format was developed that could start to match the 16 mm film equipment in both size and quality. This was the helical scan U-matic three-quarter inch tape cassette system; but with a linear speed of only 3.75 inches/second the audio quality is poor. This format is extensively used in the USA where the 16 mm film format has not gained the acceptance it has in Europe for quality programming. In Europe motion picture films for cinema release are sometimes shot in 16 mm and are of acceptable quality.

Picture quality on U-matic was originally very poor, with a band width of less than 2 MHz compared with the 5.5 MHz required for a TV broadcast system. This meant poor picture resolution and increased noise with copying. All this placed severe restrictions on the number of video generations that could be made in editing. The quality of U-matic has been improved over the years and with developments in magnetic tape a superior performance version of U-matic (SPBVA) for broadcasting became available. This format is compatible with the standard BVU format. (In Europe there is an additional BVU format called Hi-band – the high band width and low frame speed of European TV systems stretched the design of standard U-matic and a special high-resolution PAL system was produced.)

In the mid 1980s the Sony Betacam and the Matsushita/Panasonic MII video cassette system were introduced, and have overtaken the U-matic format in many situations. In Europe, they have proved to be capable of matching and emulating high quality 16 mm film production, and are rapidly taking over as a television production format. The equipment is of

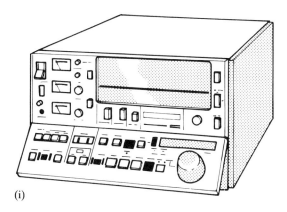

(i)

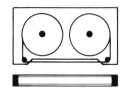

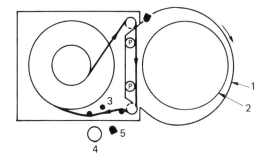

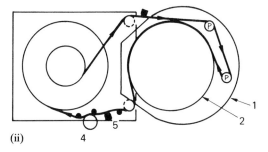

(ii)

(i) The U-matic format video cassette machine; (ii) A video cassette is inserted and the two pins (P) are rotated by the platform (1) around the video drum (2) and capstan (3) and the pinchwheel drive (4) draws the tape across the video drum, the speed of which is controlled by the pulses from the control head (5)

equal size and weight to that used in 16 mm film production. In the United States, where there is an emphasis on 35 mm film production, these formats have found less widespread acceptance.

Picture machines, used in audio post-production suites

In the audio post-production suite the U-matic video cassette recorder (VCR) has become the standard picture replay machine in most operations. Any video format can be used, but the U-matic format does provide reasonable pictures at a low outlay. Edited masters are sometimes used in audio post-production systems, and are most likely to be of the broadcast cassette format.

Unfortunately, video cassette recorders differ considerably in their mechanics and suitability for post-production.

In the film audio post-production suite, re-recording theatre, or dubbing theatre, a projector is used which is specially adapted to run at fast rewind speeds. This is, however, a compromise in design. Picture quality may suffer since fast winding speeds and high picture definition cannot be achieved in one machine.

Pictures viewed in the audio post-production suite must be easy to see, with good definition and, if projected, well lit. Video pictures can be successfully projected onto a screen up to a size of about 8 feet by 6 feet although quality is very dependent on the viewing distance. The picture definition and colour rendition is inferior to that of monitors. Although impressive, projectors do not recreate the standard domestic TV environment and the poor definition can lead to eye-strain.

To assist the re-recording mixer to accurately mix the various sound tracks of a production, a timing counter is displayed either under the screen or within it. This must be clear and easy to read. For film operations the timing counter often displays film feet, whereas for video operations a code is 'burnt into' the picture, displaying time.

Television monitors are graded according to quality, with grade 1 being used for checking broadcast transmission quality. Monitors (or projection televisions) should be capable of replaying both NTSC and PAL pictures.

Comparing film and video

Video and film are very different technologies. Film is mechanically based and comparatively simple to understand; video is dependent on more complex electronics, but both systems have their own attractions.

Film has been established for over 50 years and is made to international standards accepted throughout the world. Indeed, it was once the only medium of programme exchange in television. This has changed with the introduction of the videotape recorder, and in particular, the development of the broadcast video cassette format. Such machines are now being mass produced, at prices lower than film equipment, and with minimal operating costs (film stock, processing and printing can be expensive). Film is becoming a specialist quality format, universally used in cinemas and

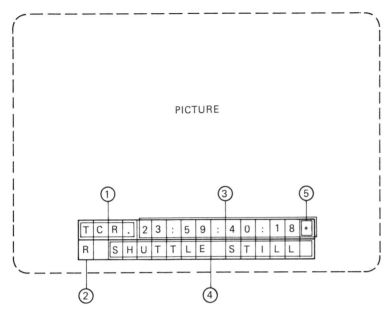

A monitor displaying 'burnt in time code' ③ in addition to video data. ① type of time data; ② videotape recorder assignment; ④ videotape recorder status; ⑤ indication of vertical interval time code

sometimes in television. In 35 mm form its image is unsurpassed in contrast ratio and definition, and the film camera will be used in quality television for many years to come.

Audio post-production offers three methods of producing a soundtrack: the film system using sprocketed magnetic film stock; the video system using a multitrack tape recorder; and to both these has been added the computer based, digital audio disc system or audio post-production workstation. All these systems use specialist equipment peculiar to the audio post-production suite.

3

Audio post-production equipment

The audio post-production process uses many specialized pieces of equipment which are not to be found in ordinary sound studios. In the film re-recording sound theatre, magnetic film recorders and reproducers are used, whereas in the video post-production area, videotape recorders are obviously needed; common to all sound recording studios are cartridge machines, disc reproducers, and tape recorders. These may or may not be modified for use in the audio post-production suite.

Video recorders and sound

Videotape recorders are optimized for video recording, not for analogue audio recording. In order to obtain a good video performance thin oxide coatings are required, but unfortunately this produces analogue audio recordings with increased distortion at low frequencies. In addition the operating speed of some video machines is particularly low, making recordings of high audio frequencies difficult. These limitations can be partially overcome with pre-emphasis and noise reduction. Worse still, some video recorders do not provide all the necessary adjustment, particularly for phase and head alignment for good audio recording.

Analogue audio performance on videotape recorders suffers from three fundamental limitations.

1. Narrow track widths are used. The 1 inch C format recorder suffers a 3.8 decibel disadvantage compared with the professional stereo audio quarter-inch machine.
2. The thin coating of videotape is optimized for scanning by rotating video heads. This means that a flux level is often necessary 10 db lower than that usually used on master quality audio recordings.
3. Very often video recording speeds are slower than audio only recorders. 1 inch C format recorders operate at 9.6 inches per second, suffering a 2 db disadvantage compared to a professional 2-track audio recorder operating at 15 inches per second. The U-matic cassette format is of notoriously low sound quality running at only 3.75 inches per second. To improve on this the Beta format uses a higher linear speed. Audio noise reduction of 4.95 inches per second is also applied to both tracks,

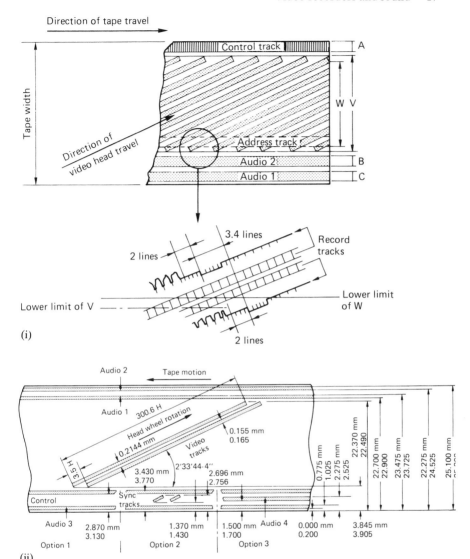

(i) The U-matic format showing both audio tracks; there is no specific time code track; (ii) The one inch format for video tape recording, options 1 & 2 provide three audio tracks (one to be time code); option 3 provides 4 audio tracks (one to be time code) (*Courtesy of Sony Broadcast and Communications*)

and in addition audio FM tracks of superior quality are available. However, these do have limited use in audio post-production and longitudinal tracks are provided with options for digital audio. Its competitor MII writes at a speed of 2.67 inches per second.

On the 1 inch C format machine there is, theoretically, a 16 db increase in noise compared to a 2-track analogue audio machine. However, noise reduction systems do improve this significantly.

The ultimate sound quality is to be found in digital recording, and this is now offered on many videotape recorder formats.

Video sound formats

Various forms of video sound format are considered in the following table:

Table 3.1 Video sound formats

Format	Tape width	Number of linear tracks	Number of digital tracks	Number of audio frequency modulation tracks
Quad	2 inch	1	–	–
C Format (NTSC American)	1 inch	2	2	–
C Format (PAL British)	1 inch	3	2	–
Beta	0.5 inch	2	–	–
Beta SP	0.5 inch	2	–	2
MII	0.5 inch	2	2	2
DI	0.5 inch	–	4	4
DII	0.5 inch	–	4	4

Audio frequency modulation recording

Originally, frequency modulation recording was developed to provide a means of producing high quality sound on domestic videotape recorders. Although not a digital system, it nevertheless produces a sound quality equal to the best professional analogue systems. The analogue signal is modulated, at a set frequency, on a carrier wave.

Frequency modulation techniques were developed after longitudinal sound recording was considered to have no more development potential on the basic video format – due to the limitations in writing speed and track width. A high writing speed is available by using the helical tracks of a videotape recorder, but since sound cannot be directly recorded on these tracks, indirect methods are used. This involves modulating the sound on to a carrier. The carrier wave is modulated by the audio frequencies, deviating up and down from its basic standing frequency. The number of times in a second it deviates is the modulation frequency, and the degree of deviation is the modulation amplitude. The recorded FM signal is not as subject to distortion or noise compared with a standard analogue recording. Nor is the frequency response dependent on the head or tape losses. The signal also tends to go into compression on overload, rather than into clipping distortion.

Audio FM recording systems are used on broadcast video cassette formats such as Betacam SP and MII. It is of very high quality, but since it can only be used when a video picture is being recorded, it has limited use in video sound editing.

Sprocketed film sound

Sprocketed magnetic film is oxide coated film of the same dimensions as camera film. Wherever possible the sound for a film production is recorded onto a separate piece of magnetic tape or film, for ease of editing and sound fidelity (this is known as double system). In the film audio post-production suite, many separate pieces of unconnected sprocketed magnetic sound film are synchronized together for mixing, to produce a final soundtrack.

Sprocketed magnetic film – 16 mm, 35 mm, 70 mm

Sixteen millimetre sprocketed magnetic film has found particular use in television productions in Europe and in other areas where 35 mm is considered too costly, (being used primarily for cinema productions). Two tracks are available on the 16 mm film sound format. In Europe the centre track is the standard monophonic track, although in America the edge track is still in current usage. Modern 16 mm machines are capable of performances close to that of 35 mm sound machines. At 25 frames per second the film runs at a speed of 7.5 inches per second.

The 35 mm soundtrack is normally positioned on the left-hand side of the film, in the same position as the soundtrack for a final print. Up to three tracks can be recorded across the film in normal usage, although it is

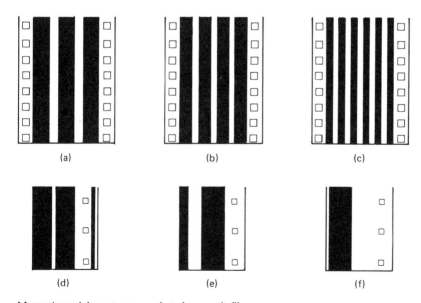

(a)   (b)   (c)

(d)   (e)   (f)

Magnetic track layouts on sprocketed magnetic film

35 mm	16 mm
a 3 track	d EBU 2 track stereo, time code
b 4 track	e 2 track edge and centre
c 6 track	f Edge track only

possible to record four or six tracks. The film runs at a speed of 18 inches per second at 24 frames per second, (occasionally, 30 frames per sec. 22.50 inches per sec.), and is capable of recording a quality equal to that of a full track, quarter-inch tape master.

The 70 mm motion picture film is rarely used, except in high cost production, and only a handful of studios are equipped to deal with it.

Sprocket drive film machines

Film is a thick and unsupple material, which is difficult to drive smoothly and accurately using the sprockets. Sprung mechanical compliance arms and dampers are used to maintain tension over the heads, whilst large flywheels reduce 'wow' and 'flutter' and sprocket modulation caused by the film's sprockets engaging or leaving the drive teeth. Some sprocket machines are driven by stepping motors, and further damping is required to reduce the pulse motion of the motor.

Capstan drive film machines

Originally, all magnetic film machines used sprocket drives to move the stock across the heads in a 'closed loop'. Nowadays, capstan drives are equally, if nct more popular, particularly if the film is to be in wind at very high speeds. In the capstan drive machine the film is driven by the capstan itself. The film sprockets only engage onto a free running sprocket wheel,

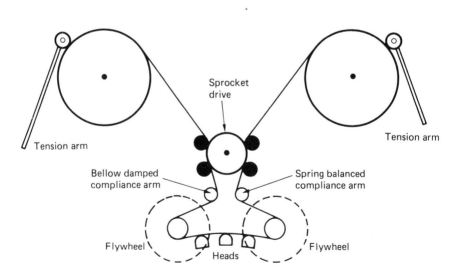

A tight loop drive system for sprocketed magnetic film, the drive is via the sprocket wheel held at two points

which monitors the speed against a reference. The capstan motor is then adjusted to correct the speed of the transport. The reference driving signal can be an external, interlock signal from a master generator, or an internal signal from a crystal oscillator. The capstan can drive the film either with the aid of a pinch wheel, known as an open loop drive or, without such assistance, using a zero loop drive. In this latter system, tension and motion sensors on both take up and supply motors, continually monitor tape speed. This speed is referred back to the films actual speed, generated from the free running sprocket wheel. The film is driven by the spooling motors, their control circuits, and nothing else.

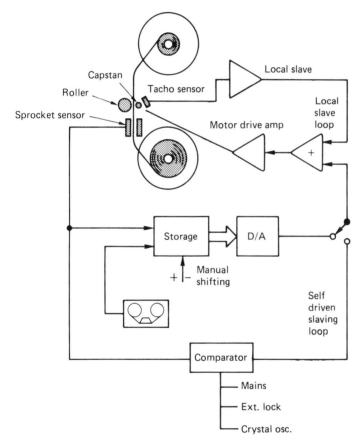

A capstan drive system for sprocketed magnetic film, a pinchwheel may or may not be used in the design

Magnetic film machines must be capable of running in synchronization with other similar machines, and facilities to slave them are always offered as part of the design. Film machines are generally driven from 'bi-phase' signals, consisting of a 5 volt, square wave signal. Other film interlock generators use mains currents or low voltage three phase signals.

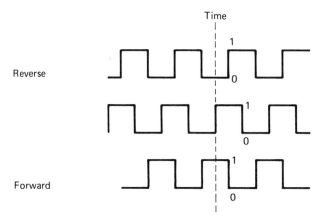

A bi-phase pulse, delivered at 5 volts square wave, producing 25 pulses per second at single speed. (see also page 56)

Requirements for sprocketed film machines

Although sprocketed film recorders are designed with audio post-production in mind, they are not exclusively used for this purpose. They are often found in television stations, locked into telecine film machines, for double system use. Telecine machines convert film images into electronic television signals, and need the facility to play a separate magnetic soundtrack with the picture. To fulfil the requirements of both audio post-production and telecine work:

1. There must be easy access to the heads for visual lining up of the 'start' synchronizing marks.
2. They should be capable of being moved remotely by frames or feet.
3. Spool tension must be such that joins are not stretched and broken.
4. They must be able to pass poorly joined film, particularly at high speed.
5. They must immediately stabilize when moving to speed or fast speed interlock from standstill. (This is far more difficult to achieve using thick sprocketed film than with audio tape.)
6. They must withdraw their heads from the stock at high speed. (Wear is more of a problem on sprocketed film than on tape.)
7. They should be capable of running loops on sound effects using magnetic film. (Modern capstan drive machines cannot do this easily.)
8. They must be capable of running stereo sound tracks without phase problems (A particular problem with 35 mm film.)
9. They should be able to accept a large variety of external synchronous signals.

Magnetic film machines should be capable of an audio performance equal to that of their equivalent counterparts which use magnetic tape. However, 'wow' and 'flutter' figures may be slightly higher, but frequency respose should be similar, particularly if the machine is designed with good head contact characteristics and polyester film is used. (This is very much more flexible than original acetate stock, and can produce higher quality results.) Sprocketed machines are expensive to manufacture and cost two to three times more than their quarter-inch counterparts. However, they are produced to universal standards and can be made to synchronize frame to frame at fast wind speeds.

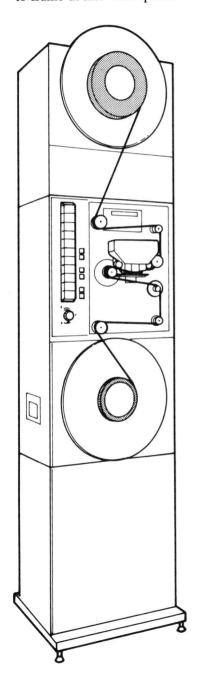

A sprocketed magnetic film machine using a capstan drive without a pinchwheel

Combined magnetic recording

It is possible to record sound in a camera onto a magnetic stripe, which is bonded to the photographic film. However, this is no longer used in professional location recording, since to provide the necessary stabilization of the film (in terms of 'wow' and 'flutter') is almost impossible due to the intermittent motion created at the picture gate. In addition, good head-to-film contact is difficult with thick uncompliant film (so this system suffers from poor frequency response). Film cameras using this system for news and current affairs programming have now been replaced by video cassette formats. However, magnetic film can have sound striped onto it, and this is used successfully on photographic cinema release prints. These are recorded using an adapted sprocketed film recorder, with special recessed heads to remove the possibility of picture scratches. They are capable of excellent results, and Dolby 70 mm, six track, stereo film soundtracks are recorded in this way.

Projectors

To view film in the audio post-production suite a special film projector is needed.

In film operations a copy is always used in audio post-production. Indeed, throughout the whole picture and sound editing process, the camera original film is never handled. Copies are called prints.

The projector must possess some additional requirements, beyond that of a standard cinema projector, in order to successfully interface with an audio post-production suite:

1. It must be compatible with the sound film transports in terms of run up, interlock, maximum rewind speeds and the control system.
2. It should not scratch or damage film, even at high speed. Although it is now very unusual to project original camera film, edited cutting copies can be easily damaged in badly designed projectors.
3. It should have a still-frame facility with a visible image, and in addition should be capable of showing an image at the highest speeds.
4. It should produce the sharpest, brightest, flicker-free image possible.

It is impossible for one machine to meet all these criteria, and two types of projectors are available for film post-production operations.

1. Those which are adapted sound film transports with prismatic or mirror projection; these machines are capable of very high speeds interlock but produce poor quality pictures.
2. Those which use cinema projection type mechanism and are only capable of running a few times normal speed, but give excellent quality pictures.

Magnetic tape recorders

Tape recorders of all varieties are used in audio post-production, but they need to be of the highest quality and in particular, must exhibit low noise characteristics to prevent the build up of background noise from multiple copying, during sound track building and mixing. Invariably, within the video post-production area, a multitrack tape recorder is used – synchronized to the videotape recorder by an electronic system called time code. This code needs to be recorded onto one of the audio tracks of the tape recorder, and this then reduces the number of soundtracks available on the machine. This is a particular problem with quarter-inch tape recorders. A 2-track, quarter-inch stereo tape machine cannot be used in stereo if one of the tracks is designated to record time code. (In America 4-track half-inch machines are often used rather than quarter-inch machines.) This problem was resolved in 1986 with the development of a new quarter-inch format, recording time code between the two audio tracks. This effectively added another track to the quarter-inch tape standard. To overcome the problems of crosstalk interference, between audio and time code within one three track head stack, most manufacturers use a separate time code record and replay head. This, however, leaves an unwanted offset between the audio recording and the time code recording. The offset is eliminated by delaying the time code signal, so that the time code is recorded in synchronization at the same point as the audio signal. The time code also needs to be delayed during replay so that the signal is synchronous for replay.

In the multitrack tape recorder, two tracks may well be taken up in providing time code information; one to provide code and the other as a guard to prevent crosstalk of the code onto adjacent tracks.

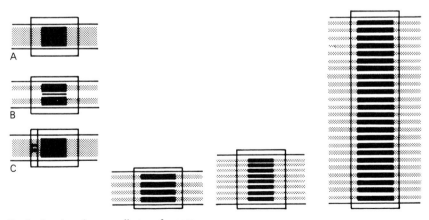

Professional analogue audio tape formats

Quarter-inch tape	Half-inch tape	One inch tape	Two inch tape
A Full track	4 track	8 track	24 track
B 2 track t/c	2 track signals	track 8 t/c	track 24 t/c
C Neo pilot with separate push-pull	1 track t/c		
recording head (for film			
synchronization, see illustration			
on page 43)			

Audio tape formats

The specifications of audio tape formats are considered in the following table:

Table 3.2 Audio tape formats

Track configuration	Tape width (inches)	Audio track width (inches)	Linear speeds (inches secs)
Mono full track	1/8	0.150	3.75
Mono full track	1/4	0.234	30/15/7.5
Stereo 2 track	1/4	0.80	30/15/7.5
Twin 2 track	1/4		30/15/7.5
Stereo 2 track	1/2	0.200	30/15
4 track	1/2	0.070	30/15
8 track	1	0.070	30/15
16 track	1	0.035	30/15
16 track	2	0.070	30/15
24 track	2	0.035	30/15

Narrow track widths on analogue tape recorders result in reduced quality. However, this can be reversed with higher tape speeds which results in reduced background noise, increased high-frequency response and reduced distortion. High speeds do have an adverse effect on bass response, but this is in general outweighed by the other aspects. High tape speeds also make editing easier.

Three professional tape speeds are used in post-production 7.5 inches per second, 15 inches per second and 30 inches per second. 15 inches per second tends to be used generally, 30 inches is more of a mastering speed, while 7.5 inches is used where maximum time is required. When multitrack recordings are made at 15 inches per second, it is not unusual to use systems to reduce background noise, whereas at speeds of 30 inches per second it may be considered unnecessary.

Noise reduction systems

Noise reduction systems work by compressing and expanding recorded sound. The overall dynamic range of the tape is restricted to a tightly controlled range during recording, so that low levels of sound on the tape are recorded at a higher level. On replay, the compressed signals are expanded up to their precise original dynamics but now, with improved background noise level. Noise reduction systems can suffer from disturbing problems of 'breathing' or 'pumping', caused when the replayed background noise from the tape is heard, varying in level, in quiet passages before and after the audio signal.

Generally speaking, most of the defects in 'compansion' systems depend on the degree of compresion used. Dropouts can also become more obvious with compansion. Three main systems are currently in use:

1. The DBX system uses a straight 2 to 1 compression expansion system.
2. The Dolby system, which splits the audio spectrum into frequency bands and uses its own separate control system, with various compression expansion ratios.
3. The Telecom system which splits the audio frequency spectrum into four bands with a 1.5 to 1 compression expansion characteristic.

Dolby SR is one of the most effective noise reduction systems available. It is far cheaper to install on an existing tape recorder than it is to purchase a new comparable digital machine, which produces a similar dynamic range. In addition, analogue recording has the advantage of a slow onset of distortion, rather than an instant breakup of the signal as is found on digital machines. However, digital sound can be copied an infinite number of times with no addition of noise, distortion or 'wow' and 'flutter'. In audio post-production where many generations of sound may be required, this can be a particular advantage.

Requirements for tape machines

In addition to being able to record sound to the highest quality and in synchronization an audio post production recorder needs to perform certain other basic functions. In audio post-production the final sound track is produced by continually updating the mix until a satisfactory version is produced. The new mix is re-recorded over the previous one, in sections or scenes; the new section being inserted by punching into record mode at an appropriate point.

To do this successfully the record switching must be silent when the 'punch in' to record is performed. In addition the 'punch in' must be 'gapless'. Film and tape recorders employ three heads in order to erase, record and replay sound. When the system enters record, normally a gap is created in the actual recording; the first head, the erase head, destroys the old recording and then the erased tape moves onto the record head, where recording starts. The gap thus created in the soundtrack is the time distance between the erase and record heads. Obviously, this is unsatisfactory and delays are employed in the erase/record switching circuitry to eliminate this problem – which occurs both on entering record and punching out of record.

Other problems associated with record synchronization are created by using separate record and replay heads. Two heads are used so as to maintain the highest audio quality and to allow the audio to be replayed during a recording for checking quality. However, one combined record replay head does have practical advantages. In audio post-production it allows the film or tape to be replayed at the same synchronous point at which it was recorded (that is with sound and picture in synchronization). If this were not so, there would be a sound lag to the picture as the tape or film replayed off the separate replay head – the spacing between the record and replay heads determining the out of sync condition. Moving or off-setting the tape or film physically, from the record to the reproducing

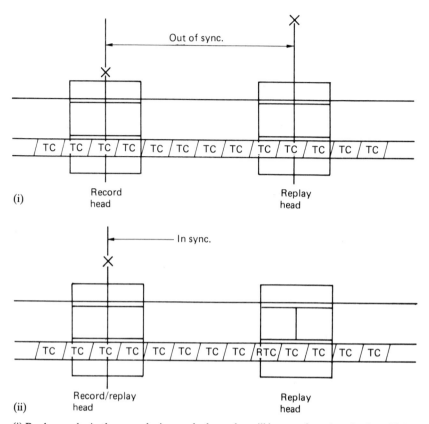

(i) Replay mode, in the reproducing mode the replay will be out of synchronization; (ii) Sync. mode, the record head can act as both a record head and a replay head, replaying synchronously (schematic layout)

head for replay, will eliminate the error. Audio post-production machines should offer high quality 'sync head' replay wherever possible.

Analogue magnetic sound and film formats are:

1. Of good quality.
2. Easy to synchronize.
3. Relatively easy to access for finding material.
4. Capable of being checked for quality while being recorded.
5. Available in various formats for different specialist purposes.

Photographic sound recording

When a videotape is played, the sound is reproduced from a magnetic sound track on the videotape. In the cinema, the sound is usually reproduced from an optical soundtrack, photographically recorded on the picture film. Optical recording is a highly specialized form of sound recording which is met in audio post-production for the cinema.

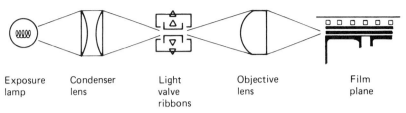

| Exposure lamp | Condenser lens | Light valve ribbons | Objective lens | Film plane |

An optical recording system used to produce a variable area sound track. The light valve ribbons move up and down within the magnetic field

To record sound photographically, light sensitive film is drawn across a slit which is formed by two metal ribbons held in a strong magnetic field. This 'light valve' open and closes as audio signals are fed into it. The light shone through this slit, traces a path onto the photographic film which varies in intensity with the signals.

This optical track is located near the edge of the film, just inside the sprocket holes (35 mm). When the film is processed and printed, the photographic image of the soundtrack is exposed as a white on black line of varying thickness. Since the areas of the black and the white within the soundtrack are continually varying, this is called a variable area soundtrack. It is now almost universally used in optical sound recording.

The soundtrack is replayed by being projected, not onto a screen but, onto a photoelectric cell which picks up the variations in light and converts them into electrical signals.

The photographic soundtrack does not reach the high fidelity standards of a magnetic film soundtrack. However, recorded optical tracks are of reasonable quality, and much of the poor sound associated with them is due to the way in which they are handled, rather than any major defect in the recording system. Many of the audio problems relate to high noise levels, which increase with use; a film soundtrack can become easily damaged as it passes through a projector. When the clear areas of the film have become scratched, they are picked up by the reproducing photo-electric cell as clicks and background hissing.

The optical soundtrack has a frequency response that is substantially flat up to 12 kHz (only an adequate figure). However, it is substantially free from compression effects at high level, and at modulations of up to 100% performs in a perfectly linear manner, this is not true of analogue magnetic recording. Various forms of equalization are used in optical recording, although none of these are in the form of pre- and post-emphasis as found in many other recording systems. If pre-emphasis were applied, there would be a danger of clipping.

The noise in an optical soundtrack is mainly in the mid-range region, caused by the granular structure of the film, and since the early 1930s noise reduction has been applied. It is described as 'ground noise reduction' and its aim is to reduce the transparent area of the track to near zero, when there is no signal. Normally, a solid state delay device is used which retards the audio fractionally, allowing the noise reduction system to 'open up' just ahead of the required programme audio (anticipating noise reduction).

Handling noise, grain noise and replay sound noise are all proportionally reduced as the width of the track is decreased. When the track is 100% opaque no noise is sent through the system, although in practice the track never completely disappears and a 'bias line' remains. Modern optical tracks are recorded with a bias line of 2 milliseconds. With suitable ground noise reduction, noise levels as low as 60 db below 100% modulation can be achieved.

To assist the recording engineer in achieving a maximum level without distortion on the optical soundtracks, two indicator lights are often provided on a recorder in addition to meters; one flashes yellow on a clash of the light valve, indicating 10 milliseconds of distortion – which is considered inaudible; one flashes red on clashes over 100 milliseconds – indicating audible distortion.

Photographic recording test procedures

To ensure that the film sound is exposed successfully, 'sensitometry tests' are made through the recording chain so as to determine:

1. The optimum exposure or the amount of light used in the optical camera.
2. The processing time needed to produce the right contrast, creating good definition between the dark and clear parts of the film, both for negative and print material.

Due to the nature of the photographic process it is impossible to obtain the ideal 100% white and 100% black intensity on a film soundtrack, so a compromise has to be reached which will produce good sound quality and low background noise. When the sound is printed onto the release print, the image should have exactly the same definition as the original camera recording. However, the system is not perfect and there is likely to be some image spread, which will result in distortion and sibilance. To optimize the processing and printing conditions film 'cross-modulation tests' are carried out.

A combined audio signal of 400 Hz and 9 kHz is recorded at various negative exposures.

Prints are produced and played off on a cross-modulation analyser. The best print will produce the highest output from the high frequencies and the lowest output from the low frequencies.

Stereo optical soundtracks are now found on most motion picture film releases. The alternative is magnetic stripe, which has to be applied after the picture has been printed and then recorded. It has been estimated that it costs ten times as much to produce a magnetic print as it does an optical release print.

The optical recording system is well suited to stereo, since two separate tracks can be easily recorded on to a photographic emulsion. A dual photo-electric cell is used to pick up the two separate outputs. These tracks are often Dolby A or SR encoded; the format being called Dolby Stereo bi-lateral Variable Area, or just Dolby SVA. The use of a sound matrix within the Dolby recording system allows four separate sources to be

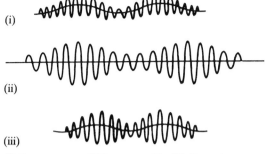

(i) Over exposure 400 hz measurable; (ii) Correct exposure 400 hz cannot be measured, no change in average transmission; (iii) Under exposure 400 hz can be measured. A high tone of 9000 hz is itself modulated at 80% at a rate of 400 times per second. The recordings are exposed at various levels and the 400 hz signal is measured

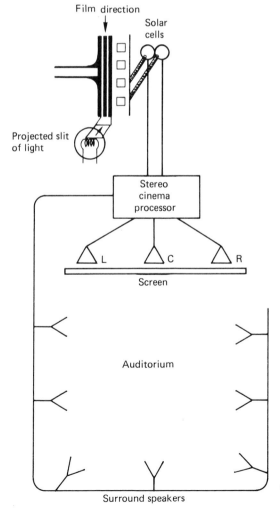

The Dolby Stereo cinema system

encoded onto the track. Three are for use behind the screen, left, centre and right, and the fourth, surround channel, is located in the audience area.

Optical sound is:

1. Easily copied by the photographic process.
2. Inherently distortion free (but goes into very heavy distortion on over-modulated peaks).
3. Susceptible to poor handling.
4. Of adequate quality.
5. Produced to universal standards.
6. Entirely mono compatible in stereo format.

4
Synchronizing audio post-production equipment

An audio post-production suite is designed to bring together the various sounds that make up a soundtrack, and allow them to be accurately mixed together into the final audio track.

The sounds may be music, effects or dialogue but all must run in synchronization with the picture, and do so repeatedly, if the sound mixer is to be able to rehearse and refine his soundtrack mix to perfection. To achieve this degree of accurate synchronization the conventional method is to use physically sprocketed film, or more recently the electronic synchronizing system called time code.

It is easy to grasp the simple mechanical principles behind sprocket synchronization; sprocketed picture film and sprocketed magnetic film soundtracks are locked together. A picture synchronizer demonstrates the system.

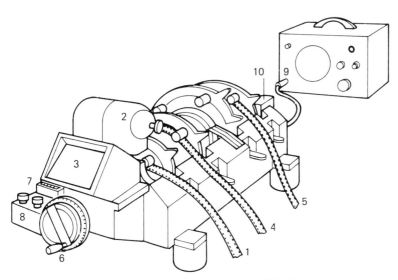

A synchronizer used for laying tracks; 1, picture track; 2, light for picture; 3, screen; 4 & 5, magnetic sound tracks; 6, crankhandle; 7, footage counter; 8, volume controls; 9, loudspeaker unit (*Courtesy of A. Nesbitt*)

Various sprocket wheels, all of the same size, are locked onto a common shaft and driven at speed, and each of the films engaging the sprocket wheel runs synchronously with the next. This is the simplest form of synchronization, but with modern electronics highly sophisticated systems are available, which are far more versatile than a simple mechanical lock. However, what happens if the recorded picture and soundtracks are not physically sprocketed? In this case an electronic sprocket is used; one originally developed for videotape editing.

Initially, videotape was edited by physically cutting the magnetic tape itself. However, this proved to be rather cumbersome since it was difficult to accurately find a particular picture frame using the electronic control track designed to synchronize the recorded picture with the revolving video drum. A poor splice resulted in the picture jumping – rather as though a bad film join had jumped in a projector gate.

Videotape editing techniques slowly improved and in the 1960s when new electronic splicing systems were introduced, these systems did not require the tape to be physically cut but worked by electronically copying the picture from one machine to another, building up the edited material by re-recording the originals into a new, edited sequence. In order to achieve this accurately, a system was needed which enabled each individual videotape picture to be identified. This identification was in the form of time, on a clock. Today, it is possible to identify the frame to be edited, enter its time or time code into the edit controller, and sit back and watch the system automatically perform a precise edit, exactly as commanded. If the edit is previewed and thought unsatisfactory, it can be trimmed, frame by frame, at will.

Time code in videotape editing gives precise time references, allows compatibility for interchange of material, and allows videotape machines to be synchronized together precisely. It is this facility that is of particular importance to audio post-production, because videotape recorders and audio tape recorders can also be synchronized together by the code.

To achieve accurate synchronization it is necessary to have special comparator circuits in each piece of audio equipment. These circuits compare all the time code readings of the various machines and adjusts their speeds to maintain synchronization. Unfortunately, until 1969 there was no standard code that could be used for synchronization, and each manufacturer had his own system. However, in 1969 it was decided to develop an international time code allowing interchangeability between systems. This code is called the Society of Motion Picture and Television Engineers/European Broadcasting Union code – abbreviated to the SMPTE/EBU code.

The SMPTE/EBU time code

Time code is recorded using a digital code. Originally used to identify frames on a videotape recorder, it can be equally useful in identifying a point on an audio tape. The code is accurate to at least one video frame in identifying a cue point for synchronization. The time span of a video frame depends on the speed of the system – not in inches per second but in frames

80 bits per frame
32 user binary spare bits
16 sync.
28 assigned address
4 unassigned address

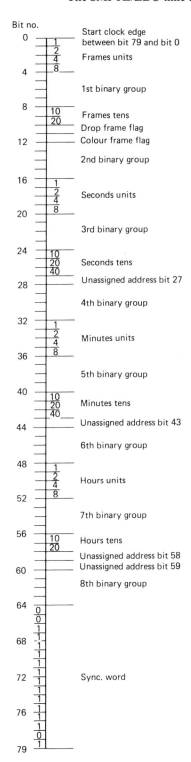

Bit no.

0 — Start clock edge between bit 79 and bit 0

1
2
4
8 — Frames units

1st binary group

10
20 — Frames tens
Drop frame flag
Colour frame flag

2nd binary group

1
2
4
8 — Seconds units

3rd binary group

10
20
40 — Seconds tens
Unassigned address bit 27

4th binary group

1
2
4
8 — Minutes units

5th binary group

10
20
40 — Minutes tens
Unassigned address bit 43

6th binary group

1
2
4
8 — Hours units

7th binary group

10
20 — Hours tens
Unassigned address bit 58
Unassigned address bit 59

8th binary group

Sync. word

The basic time code structure as recommended in EBU Technical Standard N12 1986, Time and control codes for television tape recording (*Courtesy EBU*)

per second. There can be 25 or 30 video frames in one second. Once the code has counted frames it then counts seconds, and so on, identifying up to 24 hours of frames. The code then starts again. Each frame, therefore, has its own individual second, minute and hour identification.

Each time code signal is divided into 80 pulses or bits, and each of these bits has only one or two states, on or off, referred to respectively as 'one' and 'zero'. The basic signal is a continuous stream of noughts – the signal that occurs as time code crosses midnight. However, if the signal changes its polarity halfway through a 'clock interval', the message represents a 'one'. This is a method of modulation known as bi-phrase mark encoding. If listened to it sounds like a machine-gun varying in speed, as the time progresses.

Each frame, therefore, consists of eighty parts. The speed of recording these bits will depend on the number of frames per second multiplied by eighty. Thus, in the European system there are twenty five frames each second multiplied by eighty, equalling two thousand clock rates per second. In the American system there are thirty frames per second multiplied by eighty, giving two thousand four hundred clock periods per second. This rate of bit recording is known as the clock rate or bit rate.

These coded signals are used to represent the numbers recording clock time – the time code.

| Hours | Minutes | Seconds | Frames |

Time code read in the form of an HH: MM: SS: FF display

To view a time code display it is necessary to have eight separate digits. The largest number being recorded is 23 hours, 59 minutes 59 seconds and 29 frames (USA). To reach this specific time all the numbers from 0 to 9 appear at some point, and have to be recorded. However, the code to record them is only in the form of zeros and ones.

To record numbers the code is divided into groups of four, each of the bits having only an 'On' or an 'Off' state. Bit 'One' of the group of four is designated numerical value 1 when switched on; Bit 'Two' is given the value 2; Bit 3 is given the value four; Bit 4 is given the value eight when switched on.

The chart shows the state of the Bits 1, 2, 4, 8 to represent the appropriate number. For example, to represent value 6 – Bit 1 is off; Bit 2 is on; Bit 4 is on; Bit 8 is off. Bit 2 and Bit 4 which are switched on, add up to the numerical value 6. If the number 8 is required, only Bit 4 representing 8, is, of course, switched on. Obviously, if only the numbers 1 and 2 are required – such as units of hours on the clock, a group of only 2 bits is needed; not 4 bits which extends to 8 and beyond.

A 4 bit code

Table 4.1 Chart of a 4 bit code

Decimal number	Group of 4 consecutive bits, value when switched 'on'			
	1	2	4	8
0 =	0 +	0 +	0 +	0
1 =	1 +	0 +	0 +	0
2 =	0 +	1 +	0 +	0
3 =	1 +	1 +	0 +	0
4 =	0 +	0 +	1 +	0
5 =	1 +	0 +	1 +	0
6 =	0 +	1 +	1 +	0
7 =	1 +	1 +	1 +	0
8 =	0 +	0 +	0 +	1
9 =	1 +	0 +	0 +	1
(15 =	1 +	1 +	1 +	1)

This means that using a group of four bits, any decimal number from 0 to 9 can be coded (in fact, the maximum number is 15).

The time information is spread through the 80 bit code – zero to 3, is assigned to unit frames; 8 to 9 to tens of frames; 16–19 units of seconds; 24–26 to tens of seconds; etc. Interspaced between the time information are eight groups of 4 bits each. These 26 bits are called user bits and to access their code special equipment is necessary. This information cannot be added once the code is recorded.

User bits record additional information such as the production number, the scene and take number, the identity of a camera in a multi-camera set up, and so on. The user bit information is not changed until it is programmed.

Two other user bits are available to give standard information, Bit 11 giving colour recording information to prevent flashes on edits and Bit 10 giving specific time code type information. Bits 64 to 79 are always the same in every frame, since they tell the time code encoder when the end of frame is reached and, also, if the code is running forward or backward.

Drop frame flag – bit number 10

In Europe the television system runs at exactly 25 frames per second. This is controlled by a clock, usually from a central apparatus area in a television studio. This 25 frames per second rate is extremely accurate and very critical. It is historically based on the use of a 50 cycle per second alternating current electricity generating system.

In America there is a 60 cycle generating system and this has been tied to a nominal frame rate of film at 24 frames per second. This speed was standardized when the sound film was introduced in 1928 (the slowest speed possible for apparent continuous motion). In most non-video environments this SMPTE time code is related to the 60 cycle line frequency combined with a 30 frame per second code rate. However, with the development of the NTSC colour systems it became necessary for the frame rate to be imperceptibly changed, to eliminate the possibility of crosstalk between colour information and audio. This is 0.1% lower than the nominal 30 frames per second speed. In fact, the code gradually falls behind actual real time and to maintain speed, numbers have to be dropped out of the code. Over a period of 3000 seconds, i.e. one hour, there is a loss of 3.6 seconds (0.1%). This is an error of 108 frames, and so 108 frames have to be dropped, through the hour, if real time is to be retained. To identify drop frame time code, user Bit 10 is activated. On identifying this the time code discards two frames every minute – except for every tenth minute. 60 × 2 = 120 frames per hour are admitted, except 0 10 20 30 40 50.

6 × 2 = 12 frames
Omissions = 120 − 12 which equals 108 frames per hour.

SMPTE time code, in the drop frame mode, therefore matches real time (within two frames a day). Sometimes a 30 frames per second code will be used, particularly with film. Consequently the identification of the type of time code is most important, if systems are to synchronize in post-production.

Longitudinal time code

Time code recorded on an audio track is recorded in the normal longitudinal manner (like ordinary audio) and called longitudinal time code or LTC. Using an ordinary audio replay head it is possible to recover time code information down to speeds of one-tenth of normal playing speed, or 2.5 frames per second. Unfortunately time code readings become unreliable as the tape speed approaches zero; audio output is proportional to speed, so as speed reduces to zero so output reduces to zero.
Advantages of longitudinal time code:

1. LTC is always available if a tape has been pre-striped.
2. LTC can be read at very high speeds.
3. LTC is suitable for both video and audio recording.

Disadvantages of LTC:

1. LTC cannot be accurately read in stationary mode, or inched and read at slow speeds. To overcome this, time code is often visually 'burnt into' a recorded videotape picture. This is accurate to the frame in stationary mode. (These numbers must however, to be able to be read by eye and then entered into the system via a keyboard).
2. LTC requires a track dedicated specifically to it.
3. LTC is subject to severe degradation when copied between machines and has to be reformed. This automatically happens in some equipment. (Broadcast cassette video recorders, for example).
4. LTC recording and replay circuits require special individual attention for alignment and monitoring. In addition, high speed LTC resolving is not often considered a standard requirement and is an extra on most audio equipment.

Vertical interval time code (VITC)

Vertical time code is only applicable to video recorders. It provides correct time code information when the video machine is stationary and is more useful in audio post-production because of this. Even on the highest quality broadcast recorders, the longitudinal time code track will be read inaccurately at slow speed or when stationary.

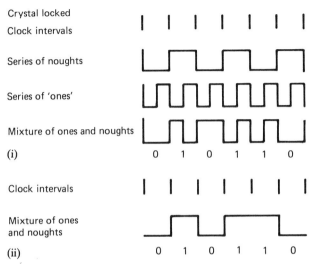

(i) The bi-phase mark modulation of longitudinal time code; (ii) Vertical interval time code, in the television system which is level responsive; a certain level represents peak white while another level represents black. The black level between the frames is used to represent 0 and a higher level nearer to white represents 1

Vertical interval time code is similar to longitudinal time code but without its own separate track. This is inserted into two unseen lines of the video picture. The pulse format which is used, does not need to be of the bi-phase type, as used in longitudinal time code. This is because there already exists within the videotape recorder system, clock information that gives accurate time reading. The modulation system used is known as a non-return to zero, or NRZ type.

For practical reasons, vertical interval time codeword has to be recorded twice. This prevents any loss of signal through 'drop-out' on the magnetic tape. If minute faults occur in the magnetic oxide in the manufacture of the tape, or through poor physical handling, there is a momentary loss of signal or a drop-out. Videotape recorders are able to detect picture drop-out and replace a faulty line with part of a previous one, thereby stopping a flash occurring on the screen. This error concealment process is hardly noticeable. It can be even used to replace damaged frames of film transferred to videotape. However imperceptible this system may be to the eye, it is not a technique that can be used on faulty time code. Replacing a time codeword with the preceding time code produces obvious inaccuracies. Instead, time code is recorded within the picture frame, more than once, as a safety precaution.

In the SMPTE system the vertical interval time code signal is inserted, not earlier than picture line 10, and not later than line 20. It is also sited in the same positions in both fields. The EBU give no specific position for VITC words, but recommend it should not be earlier than line 6 and not later than line 22.

Vertical internal time code and longitudinal time code are both met in audio post-production using video systems.

Advantages of vertical interval time code:

1. VITC is available whenever the picture video is available, even in stationary mode. This means that 'burnt in' time code may be unnecessary.
2. VITC does not require any special amplification. if the VTR can produce a good television picture it will reproduce VITC.
3. VITC does not take up what might be valuable audio track on a video tape recorder.

Disadvantages of VITC:

1. VITC cannot be read at very high spooling speeds. The individual design of the videotape recorder affects its ability to read time code at high speed. This is restricted to about twenty times normal running speed.
2. To be used successfully in audio post-production VITC has to be recorded via a transfer from the original videotape.

Midi

Midi stands for Musical instrument digital interface – a system designed for connecting various electronic instruments together, so that one instrument can control one or more of the others. It is basically a switching system. The system is used by musicians who lock together various synthesizers, in the fashion of a multitrack tape recorder, so more tracks can be recorded and more sounds built up.

The interface is fully digital and works on binary codes, which specify the type and destination of each instruction and the operational speed of the system. At least three synthesizers may be linked together before there are problems with timing. It has become a widely used and successful standard. Interfaces have now been developed to link audio post-production synchronizers and synthesizers together. The Midi interface can either be master when it generates pseudo time code, or else a slave where Midi commands are derived from time code readings.

Film time code

There is a long tradition of recording time code onto videotape, but it is unusual to find time code recorded onto photographic film. However, time code does have uses where complicated post-production is involved, and various systems have been developed.

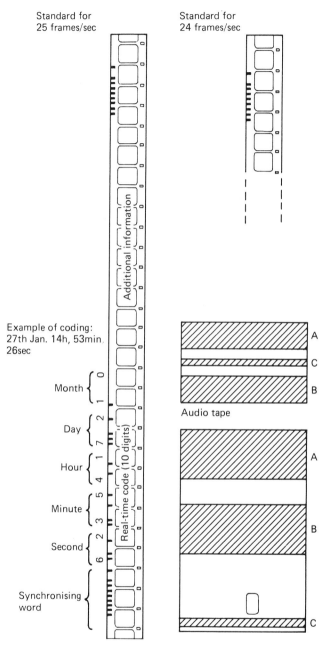

Standard for
25 frames/sec

Standard for
24 frames/sec

Example of coding:
27th Jan. 14h, 53min,
26sec

Month

Day

Hour

Minute

Second

Synchronising
word

Additional information

Real-time code (10 digits)

Audio tape

A
C
B

A

B

C

Magnetic film
Track assignments are:
(A) and (B) programme material
(C) time code

A film time code system used in Germany; there is no international time code system in film
(*Courtesy S. Bernstein*)

Aaton system

The Aaton system was specifically designed for 16 mm use. Both digital and visual readable numbers are printed onto the film stock in the camera. The system has been developed further by Panavision for use with 35 mm film. Information recorded includes, time code in digital form with visual information covering frame, scene, take, roll, production, equipment number and the date of the shooting.

Arri-VAFE system

In this system the SMPTE/EBU time code appears in digital form along the edge of the film. The system is intended for use in video-assisted filming. A video recorder is fed from an electronic viewfinder on the camera, and includes burnt-in time code from the film camera's output. This means the picture can be video-edited and then later matched to the camera negative, by means of its existing burnt-in time code.

Synchronization using sprockets

The sprocket on a photographic film is often said to fulfil the same function as time code information on videotape recorders. However, the sprocket does much more than this for it fulfils other functions.

The main purpose of the sprocket is to move the film through the camera. The sprocket wheel drives the film but, in addition, a claw mechanism engages the sprocket on the film to hold it steady for an exposure to be taken. If the sprocket wheel driving the film is locked together synchronously with other sprocket drives, various films can be run in synchronization.

By connecting a counter to the sprocket wheel driving off the moving film, it is possible to time the passage of the film. If the film is run at 24 frames per second the passing of 24 frames over the counter causes the timer to move one second. In this way frames, seconds, hours and minutes can be counted as the film passes – a form of time coding. Simple synchronizing information can be recorded onto sound tape by other methods.

Pilotone/neopilot

In film production, original recordings in the field are usually made onto a separate sound tape in synchronization with the camera. The synchronization may be controlled either with time code, or Pilotone/Neopilot pulses – both developed by the Nagra company in Switzerland.

The Pilotone and Neopilot systems synchronize by sending a train of pulses from the camera to the separate sound tape. Each pulse represents a sprocket of the camera film.

Originally, the signal was derived from a generator attached to the camera motor and sent by wire to the tape recorder. Various methods have been developed to send the pilot signal without wires, thereby allowing the camera and recorder complete freedom of operation. The generator signal can be radio transmitted from the camera to the recorder. Alternatively, the camera can be driven from a crystal oscillator which is running at the same speed as a crystal oscillator at the audio recorder – the latter producing pulses in synchronization with the camera drive.

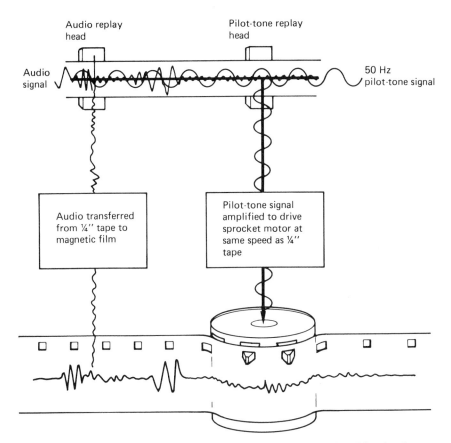

A quarter-inch to sprocketed film synchronizing system. The 50 hz synchronizing signals recorded on the location tapes are picked up at a special replay head. The pilot-tone signal is recorded in opposition to the audio signal and is 'silent' to it.

To synchronize the separate sound to the picture, the quarter-inch tape is copied onto fully coated magnetic film of the same gauge as the picture. The pulses derived from the camera motor, which are recorded on the tape, drive the motor of the film recorder holding interlock, electronic sprocket to film sprocket. The picture and sound are then matched together; editing now can take place.

The system provides a simple, effective method of synchronizing film and sound. However, the 'electronic sprocket' recording provides no time information, only synchronizing information.

Key numbers

When a photographic negative is manufactured, numbers are exposed every six inches along the edge of the material. These numbers are known as key or edge numbers. Each number uniquely identifies a piece of camera original.

When a copy is made for editing, the original numbers are duplicated with the picture on the edge of this cutting print – or in video terminology, a 'dub for off-line'. Thus the original camera negative can always be matched to the cutting print – the print being used in editing; the camera original remaining uncut. After the final edit has been completed, this cutting copy is passed to a technician known as a negative cutter. He will match the edited film to the negative by physically cutting the original masters, cut for cut, with the cutting copy. A print is then made from the cut negative. This will be free from splices or scratches and, in addition, dissolves and title-work can be added.

Example of New Edgeprint format for
EASTMAN Color Negative Films

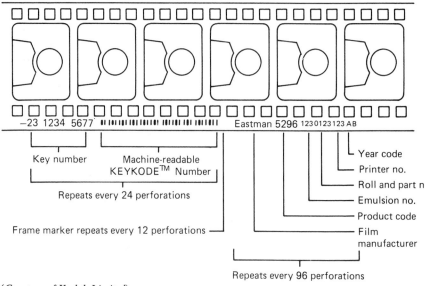

(*Courtesy of Kodak Limited*)

Rubber or frame numbers

Frame numbers are used for identifying frames during editing. Film is put through a machine which every six inches prints a unique number between the sprockets in order to identify each frame (frames being plus or minus so many sprockets, from its number). The accompanying synchronous soundtrack is also put through the machine and printed with the same synchronous numbers, thus providing synchronized information between picture and sound.

5

Recording and distributing time code

In order to record time code on a tape recorder only a limited audio band width is needed – something between 100 Hz and 10 kHz. This compares with a frequency response of 40 to 18 kHz plus or minus two decibels, for high quality audio recording. Although no special arrangements are usually made to record time code, there are problems. Analogue recorders find it difficult to record square waves, and strong, interfering, side band frequencies can be generated. This means that time code recording levels need to be chosen carefully, to minimize possible crosstalk or unwanted pickup into adjacent audio tracks. (Unfortunately, the time code wave form is at a frequency which is particularly audible.)

Crosstalk can be reduced by recording the code at a lower level. However, if the level is decreased too much, the signal will itself be susceptible to crosstalk from the adjacent audio tracks, and from the background noise of the tape itself. Typical recording levels for time code are between −6 and −15 with respect to the zero or line-up level.

If it is required to read time code at high spooling speeds, with the tape in contact with the replay head, special amplifiers with an extended frequency response are needed. It is then necessary to compensate for increased output as the speed of the tape gets faster. (In theory, at least, the recording characteristic equalization of the time code should be consistent with the speed of the tape as well!) To recover time code at up to 50 times normal speed, the replay amplifier must have a frequency

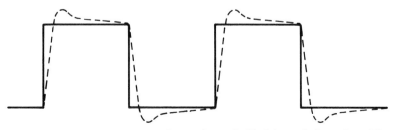

A typical time code waveform superimposed over the ideal theoretical waveform. The overshoot at the edges and the small amount of tilt is caused by phase response errors

response extending to 100 kHz. This is a difficult requirement to meet. At high tape speeds, the head to tape contact can prove to be a problem. A gap of air can build up between the head and the tape, resulting in some loss of signal.

Time code signals suffer from being copied. They should, therefore, be regenerated rather than just dubbed. Since the code consists merely of 'on' or 'off' pulses, it can be easily reconstituted.

A number of methods of improving the time code wave form are possible, depending on the severity of damage. With vertical interval time code regeneration is unnecessary, for if the video is good the VITC will also be good. However, on domestic formats such as VHS retiming and reshaping is necessary.

Reshaping time code

To reshape a poor time code waveform, a slice of the wave is first taken through the mid-amplitude point. It is then amplified and clipped, thus re-creating the new wave form. The system is simpler and more reliable than regenerating through reclocking, and is usually found as part of any time code reader.

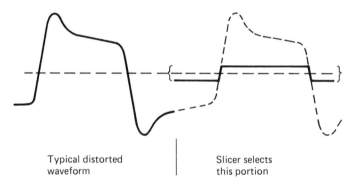

Typical distorted
waveform

Slicer selects
this portion

A time code reader in operation; the reader compares the timing between the adjacent edge pairs, the timing being taken where the signal crosses the zero line. The slice is amplified and squared up

Reclocking time code

Time code can be regenerated by reclocking; in this case a synchronous time code generator replaces bad spots in the time code which will not reshape. First, the time code generator is tied up to the faulty time code, then when the incoming code breaks up, the generator code replaces it. The system returns to the original code when it becomes good again, and this code can only be recovered at play speed.

Dedicated time code channels

Manufacturers recommend that various tracks be dedicated for longitudinal time code use.

Audio:
  Quarter-inch stereo tape recorder: bottom of track
  Quarter-inch tape recorder with centre time code: centre track
  Multitrack tape recorder: highest numbered track
  Half-inch 4 track tape recorder: track 4
  Two inch 24 track tape recorder: track 24
  16 mm film: between sprockets and edge of film
  35 mm: highest numbered track

Video:
  Two inch quad format: cue track
  One inch B format: audio track (track 3)
  One inch C format: audio track (track 3)
  U-matic high band (Europe only): dedicated time code track
  U-matic: audio track 1 outer
  Betacam SP: dedicated bottom track edge of tape
  Panasonic M2: dedicated bottom track edge of tape

Domestic VHS/Betamax:
  One of the two audio tracks

Distributing time code

Various terms are used to describe the methods of distributing time code and data information. The technical jargon that has developed often appears to have been designed, specifically, to confuse the uninitiated as well as to enlighten those 'in the know'. However, it is basically simple to understand.

Bus

A bus is a point from which various sources can be taken. In a synchronizing system, for example, it is the line of outputs from where time code is sent to the various slave tape recorders. More slaves can be added from this time code bus, if required.

Interface

This is the point at which the slave machines and bus meet. The interface is the connection or meeting point of two systems. An interface with its machine combination is known as a tributary.

Port

This is the means whereby an interface connects to a bus. A port is an outlet or an inlet. The output from an audio machine controller is called a

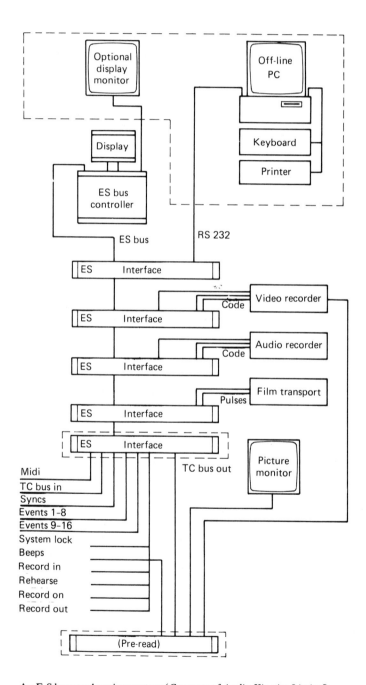

An E-S bus synchronizer system (*Courtesy of Audio Kinetics Limited*)

port, is being commanded by a time code, with an interface connecting to the audio machine via a bus.

RS232 and RS422 ports

These are specific ports for computers. Much audio post-production equipment is fitted with a socket or port to connect it to a computer, perhaps a personal computer (a PC). The RS numbers refer to recommended standards drawn up by the Electronic Industries Association of America. The full form of the reference includes a letter to indicate the current revision of the code, RS232C being the third version. The standards basically related to the mechanical and electrical specifications of the pins of the socket.

RS232 is a 'current loop system' driven by supply voltage of plus or minus 12 volts to ground, whereas, RS423 is approximately plus or minus 5 volts to ground. RS423 is designed for balanced lines, giving the advantages of long working distances and better noise rejection. These ports can either be used in parallel where any basic functions are available, or in serial form, where all the functions are available. The ports can be used with various different codes and protocols.

Protocols

In diplomatic circles this describes a draft document. It now applies to agreed specifications for communications systems such as the E–S bus.

E–S bus

The European Broadcasting Union (EBU) and the Society of Motion Picture and Television Engineers (SMPTE) have produced a specification for a digital remote control system using interfaces on a common bus, EBU TECH. 33245-E or ANSI-SMPTE 207M. This specification has become known as EBU SMPTE bus or E–S bus. It uses the RS422 electrical standard and carries information at 38.4K bits per second. It allows any manufactured synchronizer with an E–S bus specification to control any machine (with an E–S bus specification) via the bus. This ideal, universal system has tremendous complexity; it will never be complete simply because there are many facilities specific to individual manufacturers that do not appear on the bus specification. The messages that control the operation of the individual machines are called machine dialects (commands). The E–S bus system specifies standard interfaces to control video machines, audio recorders and sprocketed film machines.

The advantages of this distributed intelligence system are that:

1. It allows easy reconfiguration of the system, without affecting other users.
2. It works quickly.
3. It is less likely to fail since most failures are localized.
4. The control system is independent of the type of equipment used.

6

Synchronizers and controllers

The heart of any audio post-production system whether film or video is the synchronizer and its control unit. From here the various pieces of picture and sound equipment are made to run together in synchronization. In fact any individual piece of audio post-production equipment can be synchronized with another, providing the material has time code recorded on it, is pulse coded, or is physically sprocketed. It does not matter if the synchronizing systems are different. If the synchronizing information is available and accurate, synchronization is possible. Film sound and picture equipment can, for example, be locked to non-sprocketed, time coded, tape recordings (as often happens with music recordings) although usually magnetic film will be used in film production, and tape in video productions.

It is not unusual, in film audio work for one manufacturer to supply all the necessary equipment together with the synchronizer (this is a tradition that began at the onset of sound motion picture production, with such companies in America, as Western Electric and RCA). In contrast to this video post-production systems have been developed from equipment already available, synchronizers are, therefore, more complicated, needing to interface with many different manufacturers' designs.

Essentially, therefore, a synchronizer and its associated controller enable sound and picture transports to run up to playing speed and into synchronization. In addition, they enable equipment to be interlocked at fast forward, reverse speeds and slow speeds. When equipment is running backwards and forwards in synchronization, for preview or rehearsal, it is said to be running in 'rock and roll' mode.

To keep the machines in synchronization together special motor control circuits are used.

Servo control of transports

Tape and most film transport drives, are synchronized by servo control systems. The drive motors receive their synchronizing information from time code recorded on the tape or, alternatively, from a free-running tachometer wheel driven by the sprockets of the magnetic film. These time code or sprocket pulses are then referred to an incoming master signal. The machines speed is then continuously altered, to match the exact speed of the incoming signal. This is called a 'closed loop' servo system, so the precise speed of the transport is slaved to an outside source. In this way many transports can be run-up together, in synchronization, with their varying speed and direction controlled from the master source.

Tape recorder synchronizers have to be able to accommodate a number of different motor control systems from different manufacturers. These are usually frequency controlled (4.8 kHz to 19.2 kHz) but they can be DC voltage controlled (4 volts to 24 volts).

Various terms are used to describe the machines and methods of synchronization used for controlling audio post-production systems. At the centre is the master machine. The speed of the master is not controlled by the synchronizer, it simply produces either time code or sprocket pulses, for the rest of the system to follow and slave to.

Master

Normally, in video audio post-production the videotape is the master and is operated, either manually from its own controls or from the synchronizer controls. Videotape recorders are far more difficult to control from

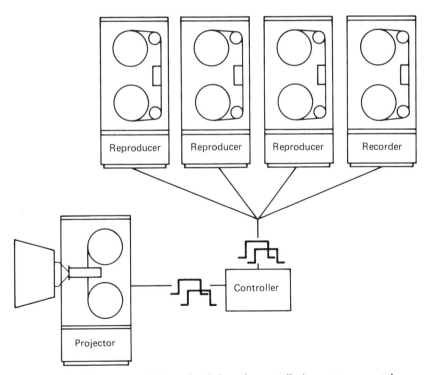

A film synchronizing system, bi-phase signals from the controller/generator are sent the projector and the sprocketed film transports. The signals provide total transport control of direction and speed

external sources, as slaves, than audio tape recorders. The most important aspect of the slave machine is its ability to vary its capstan speed, and so locate synchronously when in play. Most audio machines can provide variations of between half and twice the speed for this. Videotape recorders cannot vary their speed to any such extent.

In film systems the projector is often the master, although a central generator can be used, when the projector operates as merely another slave, with no additional synchronizing problems.

Slave

A slave is a machine which is forced to run in synchronization with the master. These are usually audio tape recorders, or sprocketed film sound machines. They chase a known time code or pulse chain. To examine the efficiency of a synchronized slave, it is important to know both its synchronous resolution and its lock-up time. Using too close (hard) a lock will result in the audio machine picking up the speed fluctuation from the master. Normally, a softer lock is used which, although staying within reasonable synchronizing limits, is not affected by the 'wow' and 'flutter' of the master machine. The synchronous resolution defines the limits to which the system will normally synchronize. A synchronizing slave will not synchronize exactly – it will tend to lag behind. This lag can range from one frame to sub-frame resolution of 1/80th of 1/100th of a frame. However, these figures apply only when the master and tape slaves are in motion. There is no synchronization when tape machines are stationary; film machines, however, always stop in synchronization.

The lock up, or synchronizing time defines the period it takes for the master and slaves to reach synchronization. It should be defined within three parameters:

1. The time synchronous resolution is achieved.
2. The time specified 'wow' and 'flutter' is achieved.
3. The lock time against fast wind speeds, the most crucial operation being the time taken from fast rewind to single speed forwards.

Chase synchronizer

The simplest of synchronizers is the chase unit usually controlling one slave machine, this slave is under synchronizer control and simply follows or chases the master wherever it goes. In a time code system the master time code, is fed into the chase unit, together with the time code from the slave. The two are then compared and the slave's speed is adjusted to match that of the master. This works quite satisfactorily at single speed forward, where the tape is under the control of the capstan motor. However, when the slave tape recorder is commanded to go faster by the master, problems begin to appear. At a certain speed the capstan drive will be unable to drive the slave fast enough. The transport must now disengage the drive capstan and switch into spooling mode. However, the speed can no longer be carefully controlled and monitored; fast spooling is usually uncontrolled and at a random speed. The slave may then run wildly away from the time code on the master. This will result in synchronization taking an excessively long time when the master returns to play speed. To combat this, special tape recorders have been developed which are capable of controlling and monitoring spooling speeds when in chase mode.

Magnetic film machines do not disengage their sprocket drives when running at high speed. Such machines, (manufactured with their own chase synchronizer built in) run in frame to frame lock-up to speeds of thirty times normal in any direction. Hence, at all speeds, they act as true slaves and as such, have exceptionally fast synchronizing lock-up times. Any number of slave machines can be driven from one master generator.

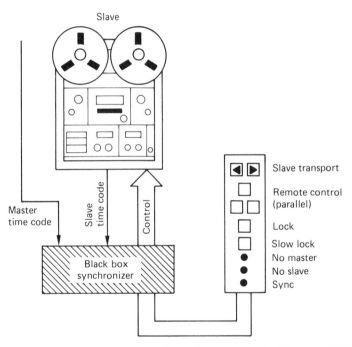

A 'black box' synchronizer controlling a slave tape recorder (*Courtesy of F W O Bauch Limited and Studer Revox*)

When only one tape machine is required to follow a master video machine a chase synchronizer may be the ideal device to use. However, when more than one slave is needed a multi-machine synchronizer may be more suitable. This can increase synchronizing efficiency, as well as providing remote controls for all the machines. These multi-machine devices can interface with most types of slave tape recorders that are available, each machine being provided with its own chase unit within the synchronizer's electronics.

A chase synchronizer will only respond to the last data presented to it. When controlling a slave it has always to wait for the master. The slave cannot be told to park until the master has stopped and told the synchronizer the park point. This takes time, and to increase the efficiency of tape systems, control synchronization is often used – here the master is under the control of the synchronizer.

Control synchronizers

In a control synchronizer all the machines, master and slaves are connected to the central controller. This incorporates a keyboard for addressing location points. The video master is now no longer put into play or fast wind to find a cue point; rather, the cue point is fed into the keyboard. The slaves and the master are then instructed to go to that address. They do this individually, in fast wind, in their own time. On reaching the address point the machines revert to a master–slave, chase status and synchronization carries on normally.

For the system to work successfully it is essential that the controller is addressed with location points, otherwise the system will, of course, revert to chase mode.

Intelligent synchronizers

The control synchronizer can be further developed to produce an even more sophisticated system of transport control known as the intelligent synchronizer. This actually remembers the way in which each machine under its control responds to commands. The commands are then modified to speed up operations.

Some synchronizers for example, park at a set time, namely the pre-roll time, ahead of an address. This allows the machines to run up to speed prior to the address point. Intelligent synchronizers will automatically reduce this pre-roll time, to the actual run-up time of the slowest machine thereby speeding up operations.

Some intelligent synchronizers use an autolock system. This is a synchronizing mode which is a compromise between frame lock, where the slaves are locked to the master, and sync lock, where a machine is locked to an external generator. In auto lock, to get the best of both worlds, the machines run-up on frame lock to within 1/100th of a frame. They then automatically revert to sync lock. This reduces any changes of 'wow' and 'flutter' being introduced from the master, whose time code is produced from a moving transport which has its own inherent 'wow' and 'flutter' problems.

For a synchronizer to work successfully at high speeds, time code must be read accurately from both master and slaves. Longitudinal time code can be read at high speed, but this does require special tape heads and wide frequency range replay amplifiers. The tape heads need to be held in contact with the tape all the time, and this can accelerate head wear. This can prove to be expensive in the case of multitrack machines.

Tachometer control

To eliminate these problems information, from the tape roller which provides the footage counter information, is used to produce pseudo time code. The slave system now deals only with time code at, or near play speed. High speed information comes from the time counter which has in addition, a direction indicator. These signals are normally produced by two optical sensors which are 90 degrees out of phase. The sensors lie in the path of a punched disc, driven by a tape roller. One of the sensors provides speed information and, by comparing its phase relationship to the second signal, direction can be detected. (Within the machine this information is used as part of the auto-locator). The tachometer pulse frequency is a square wave, similar to a film bi-phase synchronizing pulse, operating at a speed from a few hertz upwards.

But using tachometer pulses creates its own problems. Small deviations within the mechanics of the system can lead to errors of two, or three seconds, over five minutes of spooling. This will slow synchronization when play speed is reached. Additionally, tachometer control will, unfortunately, only work where the time code on the tape has been recorded continuously. It cannot be used for synchronizing material with discontinuous code.

When a synchronizer switches from reading time code to tachometer pulses, for high speed operation, the tachometer is set against the last time code reading. The synchronizer then counts 'pseudo time code', up or down, from this time code point. No reference is made to the actual time code on the tape. The actual time code ought to be continuous but could skip, repeat, or even stop. However, the synchronizer will have no knowledge of this until it reverts to reading time code at normal speed, when the difference between slave and master code will be apparent. At this point the system attempts synchronization again, probably reverting to spooling mode and further errors. It is essential, therefore, in tachometer systems to use continuous time code. In synchronizing discontinuous tapes at high speed, it is essential to use high speed time code readers. These find particular applications in synchronizing location videotapes with separate sound tapes. Tachometer systems are quite satisfactory in studio situations. They are entirely unnecessary on magnetic film machines where the sprockets deliver accurate speed information in all conditions.

Film synchronizers

Sprocketed magnetic film machines synchronize simply by chasing a master. Normally, the remote control unit or alternatively the master machine, the projector, will send master synchronizing information to the slaves in the form of bi-phase pulses. These are similar to tachometer pulses.

The train of sprocket pulses are coded to indicate direction, and vary in speed with the speed of the master. Modern sprocket drive machines are under total transport control.

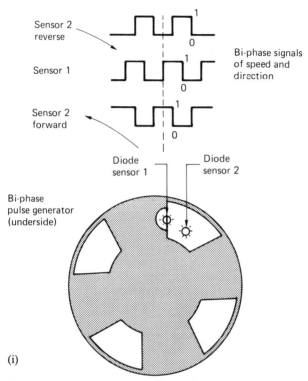

(i) A tachometer generator containing light emitting and receiving diode sensors, this type of generator is also used to provide bi-phase speed and direction pulses to control and synchronize sprocketed film transports and can also provide tachometer pulses if fitted to audio tape recorders for autolocating (*Courtesy of F W O Bauch Limited and Studer/Revox*)

Operational functions of controllers

A basic chase synchronizer is merely an electronic synchronizing box and as such it offers no operational facilities at all. All instructions come from the master machine, which may well be operated from remote switching in the mixing room. These remote switching units are generally called 'controllers'.

The basic function of any controller, such as is found in a film re-recording theatre, is to provide motion control. This covers single speed forward, fast forward, fast reverse, and single speed reverse with an additional device for inching during picture search, and switching into record.

Controllers can provide the following features which are useful in both film and video systems.

A cycle or loop facility:
The system sets up and repeats a play–rewind–play, sequence between points which are held in the memory. It is used in Automatic Dialogue Replacement.

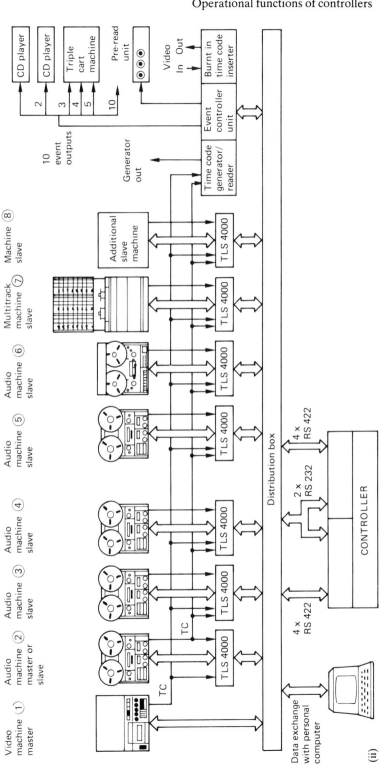

(ii) A multi machine audio post-production system with each machine having its own slave synchronizer (TLS4000) with an RS323/RS422 interface to the controller (*Courtesy of F W O Bauch Limited and Studer/Revox*)

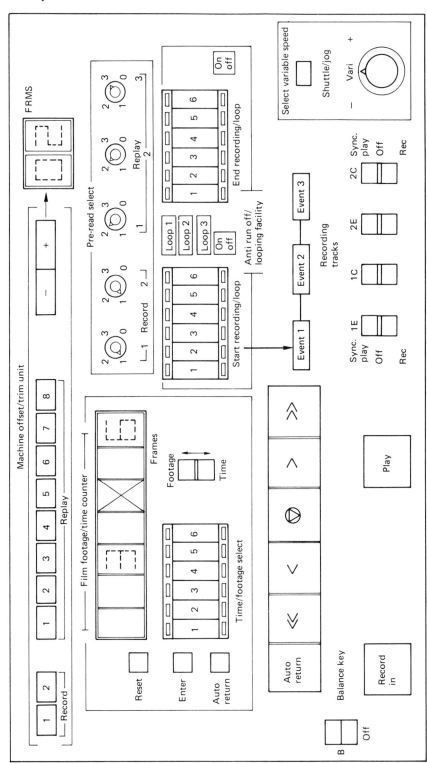

Offsets:
    These occur when a master and slave are running in synchronization but
    with different time codes; or in film where the tracks have been moved
    relative to each other. The facility should allow for an automatic return
    to synchronization with the offset calculation remembered.
Trim or Inching:
    This applies to small offsets of frames when machines are individually
    moved, usually with a trim button.
Automatic Return:
    Automatic Return to last locate position.
Events Control:
    The automatic start and stopping of external devices such as record start
    and stop and tape recorders and triggering of discs etc.
Security Anti-Run-Off:
    Stopping the machines running off the ends of reels in high speed mode.
Movable Zero:
    This facility allows the time code counter or footage counter to run from
    zero at any desired point.

Audio, video post-production controllers using multitrack tape recorders have certain additional facilities not necessarily required for film
systems.

Machine Selector:
    In this mode a switching sequence is available to re-assign slaves and
    masters. This permits any combination of the machines to be slave or
    master. The controller should also allow any machine, on its own, to be
    addressed by the controller.
Pre-roll:
    When machines are put into play, synchronism is achieved during the
    pre-roll time. This is calculated at a point earlier than the actual address
    time. It can take into account the varying run-up times of the machines.
Instant Replay
    This gives us a review of the immediate past section of the tape. Length
    of roll-back can be varied depending on the operational needs taking
    into account machine run-up and stabilizing times.
Lock Variations
    Some controllers offer variations in the type and speed of locking. The
    choice is between locking on code, on tach, on an external generator or
    on frame information. Some controllers offer variations in lock-up times
    as well.
Out of Sync Alarm
    Lights should indicate when any machine is 'out of sync' or 'in sync'.

Digital audio disc post-production systems

The most modern development of the audio post-production controller is
found in the digital audio workstation. Here audio sound is manipulated in
the digital domain on computer data discs. The system unifies all the stages
of film and video sound post-production together. It performs all the

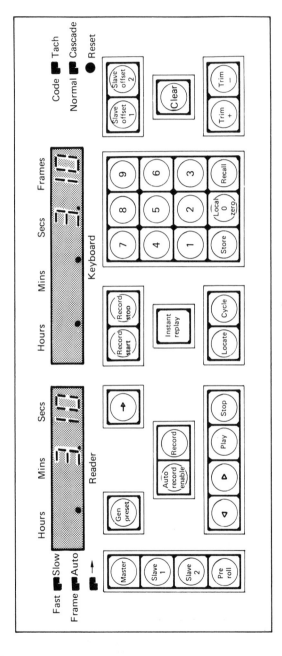

A control panel which includes a visual display unit (*Permission of Audio Kinetics UK Limited*)

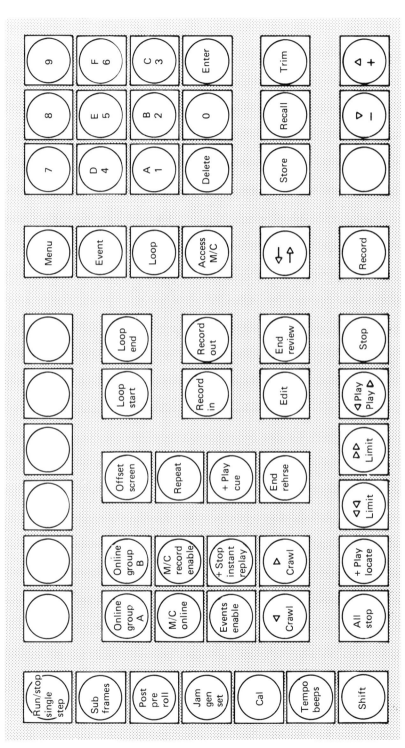

A control panel for an audio post-production video/multitrack tape recorder system, not using a visual display monitor (*Permission of Audio Kinetics UK Limited*)

normal functions of a synchronizing controller, but may also include an audio console for mixing the sounds together. These total systems can offer such features as:

1. Manipulating sound entirely within the digital domain.
2. A multi-channel mixer, complete with automated facilities.
3. A video display unit graphically showing the status of the control soundtracks.
4. A visual display unit with active graphics showing the complete status of the system during editing and the status of the mixing console.
5. Visual displays of sound modulation to aid editing.
6. Analogue to digital converters in order to allow all normal equipment to be interfaced with the system, both video and audio.
7. Time code and pulse synchronizing systems for locking of the external video and audio machines.
8. Piano type keyboards for triggering sounds.

Requirements of analogue tape recorders suitable for audio post-production synchronizers

Audio post-production tape machines should have the following facilities in order to enable them to run successfully in synchronization with other machines:

1. Fast controlled run-up times from standstill. If a machine is slow to reach speed without the control of a synchronizer, it will be even slower when controlled by a synchronizer. This usually means a low inertia capstan drive system.
2. Standard interface boards and cable should be available to allow the machine to be easily connected to its synchronizer. This means the machine will have its own auto-locator.
3. It should be possible, if required, for the machine to read time code from the time code head in a fast rewind mode. Separate high speed time code amplifiers should be available.
4. All tracks should be capable of being selected individually by remote control.
5. The machine should be capable of playing off the record head with high quality, to allow sounds to be 'bounced' between tracks.
6. The machine should automatically fall back onto input mode after recording stops.
7. The crosstalk should be minimal, even on adjacent tracks on a multitrack machine.
8. The machine should have the ability to run in reverse at single speed under control, and crawl at slow speed.
9. The machine should have available an extended tape path, allowing a pre-head to be fitted upstream of the replay head, to feed a cueing device giving a countdown of audio signals to be replayed.
10. When the machine is under remote control is should operate its transport functions with the same speed at every command. Thus if an

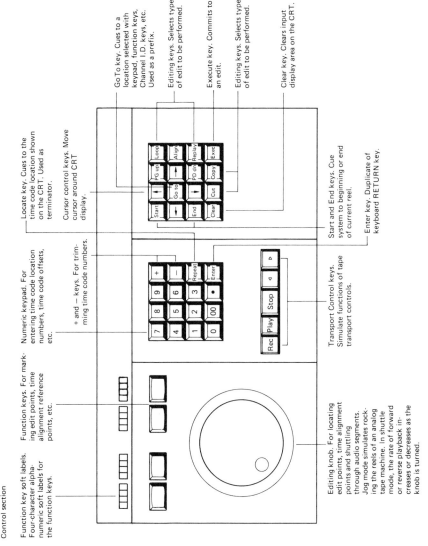

Control section

Function key soft labels. Four-character alpha-numeric soft labels for the function keys.

Function keys. For marking edit points, time alignment reference points, etc.

Numeric keypad. For entering time code location numbers, time code offsets, etc.

+ and − keys. For trimming time code numbers.

Editing knob. For locating edit points, time alignment points and shuttling through audio segments. Jog mode simulates rocking the reels of an analog tape machine. In shuttle mode, the rate of forward or reverse playback increases or decreases as the knob is turned.

Transport Control keys. Simulate functions of tape transport controls.

Locate key. Cues to the time code location shown on the CRT. Used as terminator.

Cursor control keys. Move cursor around CRT display.

Go To key. Cues to a location selected with keypad, function keys, Channel I.D. keys, etc. Used as a prefix.

Editing keys. Selects type of edit to be performed.

Execute key. Commits to an edit.

Editing keys. Selects type of edit to be performed.

Clear key. Clears input display area on the CRT.

Start and End keys. Cue system to beginning or end of current reel.

Enter key. Duplicate of keyboard RETURN key.

A workstation controller (*Courtesy of F W O Bauch Limited and Lexicon Opus*)

intelligent synchronizer is monitoring these functions, and remembering the machine's ballistics, it will be capable of controlling the machine with greater accuracy.

11. It should be FM servo controlled for speedy, accurate synchronization.
12. Centre time code, quarter-inch machines should have time compensated delay circuits, to allow time code recorded at the record head to be replayed at the correct synchronizing point.

Requirements of video tape recorders suitable for post-production synchronizers

1. To deliver tach pulses in all wind modes.
2. To reach play speed quickly and smoothly from any previous mode, so as to assist synchronization with the audio machines.
3. To run at play with as little 'wow' and 'flutter' as possible.
4. To run in single speed reverse.
5. To jog picture for search and cueing.
6. To deliver usable time code in any mode.
7. To read time code successfully at high speed if required.
8. To play off vertical interval time code if required.
9. To automatically unlace the head drum, if stationary after a set time, and so reduce the possibility of tape damage and wear – particularly if picture masters are being used.
10. To run at high speed in contact with the head, producing good pictures (up to at least 30 times, is possible) in all modes.
11. To offer remote control of all facilities required.
12. To offer excellent audio recording quality if the recorder is to be used as a master recorder.
13. To play back both NTSC and PAL videotapes.

Problems with time code synchronization

There are several problems associated with time code synchronization.
If a slave machine is running wild when selected, check:

1. The machine is selected to external drive.
2. The machine has been run to load the synchronizer with its time code at the correct speed (tachometer controlled machines).
3. The time code and audio material are at the same speed, particularly on prestriped tapes.
4. If a 'go to' position has been loaded into the controller.
5. Heeere is no unwanted offset in slave memory.
6. The time code is continuous.
7. The time code is present.

If time code is not being read correctly, check:

1. If the heads are dirty.
2. If the time code is re-copied and of poor quality; (second generation will not read at high speed).

3. If the time code is at the correct frame rate, and speed.
4. If the time code is at a usable level.
5. If the memory does not include an unwanted offset.

If a slave runs in the wrong direction, check:

1. If the time code has crossed midnight (00:00:00:00); (some synchronizers cannot tell direction across midnight).
2. If the time code is ascending and that discontinuous time code numbers are not being repeated within a roll.
3. The wind limits (anti run off). If the machine is outside the window of wind limits, it may try to locate by going past midnight.

7

Digital sound in audio post-production

The principle and practices of digital audio recording have little or nothing to do with past traditions of analogue audio. They are much more akin to today's computer technology, rather than audio engineering.

Although a 15 inches second analogue audio tape recording can, with noise reduction, produce a very high quality sound recording, it is not perfect. The distortion is in the order of several per cent at near peak and audible, while background noise is comparatively high and modulation noise is clearly noticeable when sounds, such as keys rattling and telephone bells, are recorded.

Unlike analogue recording where the actual recording medium limits quality, within the digital audio recording system there are no limitations. In digital audio the dynamic range is only controlled by the number of digital bits recorded. There is no degradation of the signal in copying, no modulation noise, no distortion, no 'wow' and 'flutter', and no print-through. For the first time in the history of recording, almost perfect audio recordings can be made. The quality problems of digital recording are now concerned with the conversion of the signal, from analogue to digital and from digital to analogue.

Digital signals require to be recorded at a much higher density than their analogue counterparts. No longer does the frequency response of the system merely need to reach 20 kHz. Now it must reach several megahertz. The band width for a digital recorder needs to be something in the region of 30 times greater than for an analogue recorder.

In a tape recording system the maximum frequency that can be recorded will depend upon the tape speed across the head, and the head gap. The problems of recording very high frequencies can be solved in three ways:

1. By using stationary head and moving the tape across it at a very high speed.
2. By using a system of multitrack heads which split the data into different channels.
3. By using rotating heads and low tape speeds so creating a high writing speed on the tape itself, in the manner of videotape recording.

Systems 2 and 3 are used by various manufacturers to record audio digitally but, unfortunately, to various differing standards.

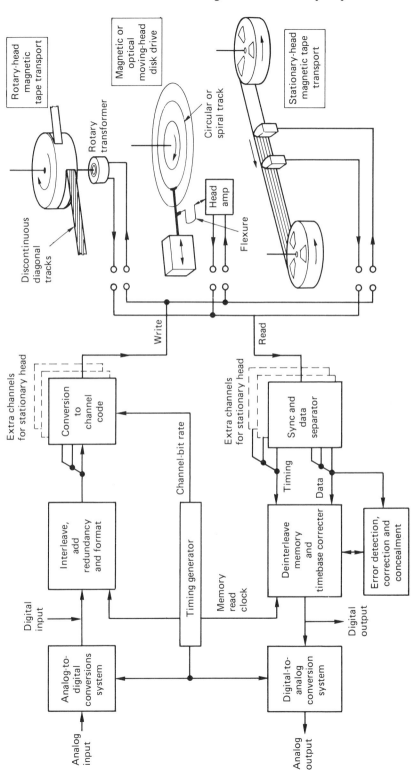

The basic digital recording system showing the rotary tape transport, the disc transport and the linear transport (*From J Watkinson, The Art of Digital Audio, by permission*)

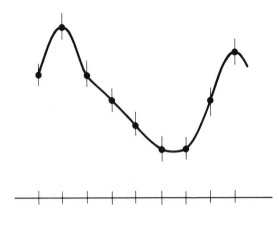

An analogue signal is sampled
at equal intervals

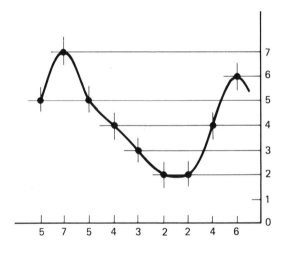

The sample signal is then
quantized

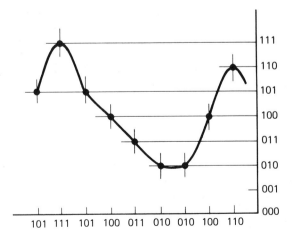

The quantized signal is then
digitized, in this example
using a simple 3 bit system

Principle of digital recording

In order to record sound digitally, three successive steps are needed to 'encode' the material. The incoming signal is first sampled at regular intervals, and the magnitude is determined.

These samples are then quantified by giving each a quantity value, from a set of spaced values, so that the original signal can be represented by a string of numbers.

In the third and final step, the numbers are converted to form binary digits. By these three steps, the original signal can now be represented by a series of digits. Each sample is called a word, and in the example shown has three binary digital bits. The recording consists of a string of data bits, similar to those used in time code.

Recording digital audio

The digital signals take either one or two possible values. In recorded form these will become equally saturated points of magnetization – one positive and one negative. Noise within the system can be completely ignored, providing that the two values have not been so degraded that they are lost in this background noise.

When the original analogue sound is sampled, the sampling must take place at precisely regular intervals, as any errors will introduce 'wow' and 'flutter' into the recording or reproduction. Unfortunately, drop-out (a momentary loss in signal) is possible in magnetic recording and since this could destroy part of the continuous signal of pulses, the system must be designed to check itself (rather as vertical interval time code restores and checks itself on a videotape recorder).

Sampling rate

The sampling rate of a digital sound recording system is normally greater than twice the highest frequency to be recorded. In audio recording the sampling rate must exceed 40 kHz, but the audio frequencies outside half this band-width must be eliminated before coding takes place (aliasing) otherwise spurious audible signals will be heard in the final decoded sound. Half the sampling signal is called 'a nyquist frequency'.

Quantizing level

It is the quantizing process that determines the signal to noise ratio of the system c⁻ the depth of the noise of the system (the quality of noise is very different from that of the analogue system). It is possible, in certain very critical conditions, to hear the background level 'falling off' when the 'floor depth' of the dynamic range is reached.

Digital band width

The band width, or range of frequencies, required to record a digital signal is the product of the sampling rate and the number of bits per word. If the sampling rate exceeds 40 kHz in a 16 bit system (considered the minimum possible for quality recording), the band width will have to be at least 640 kHz to include all the necessary error correction, a band width of 1.5 mHz is more practical.

Memories

To record digital information, whether or not it be audio signals, a recording system or a memory is required. This could be a spool of tape, a magnetic computer disc or a semiconductor integrated circuit.

ROM

If a memory is recorded once and can only then be replayed, it is classified as a ROM – a read only memory. This term usually applies to integrated circuit semi-conductor devices, whose memory is permanently built-in during manufacture.

EPROM

This is distinguished from the ROM in that the EPROM, or erasable programmable read only memory, can be programmed by the user. It, too, can come in the form of an integrated circuit.

RAM

Faster than these memories is the random access memory which is a read and write memory, once again, in the form of solid state semiconductors. Although this has excellent access it has little storage capacity, and only seconds can be stored at time.

Disc drives

To record more than a few seconds of digital data into a solid state memory with no moving parts is technically difficult, and other methods have to be used for recording long passages of digital audio.

The magnetic computer disc provides an answer to this problem, offering good storage capacity and excellent access to the recorded information. Two forms of disc are available, floppy discs and hard discs. In floppy discs the magnetic recording medium is flexible, with the recording head touching it. These are cheap to manufacture but have a very small capacity (100 kilobytes upwards to a few megabytes). Their use is limited to only recording small samples of audio, as well as filing information, such as edit lists, and console set-up details. The hard computer disc, however, has excellent storage capacity and systems are available that can record hours of magnetically recorded digital sound, with almost instant access. The circular magnetic tracks on the disc's surface repeatedly present data to the replay head. The rotational speed of the disc determines the access time. The universally used Winchester disc system provides particularly good access since the height of the head above the disc is reduced to a minimum, in order to increase the capacity, and the head can move to a point on the disc within a few tenths of a millisecond – a negligible time for audio purposes. Since the disc, disc head and positioners are in a sealed unit, away from contamination, the disc cannot be removed from the disc package.

About thirty minutes of digital audio can be held on a disc (200 megabytes capacity). When used in conjunction with a solid state random access memory device, a single disc drive can access several different tracks at once and can appear to have many tracks playing at the same time. The system only records that part of the soundtrack which contains the audio; if there is silence no more storage space is taken up on the disc. Since there is no fixed physical relationship, between the different tracks, as there is on a multitrack tape recorder, it is easy to move the tracks relative to each other.

In audio post-production it is often necessary to hear audio at higher than normal speeds to quickly find cues. By simply increasing the digital system's clock frequency, the drive will run faster. This will only work at a little above normal speed, and in order to go still faster, special files of spooling audio are memorized when the original recordings are made.

One advantage of the disc based audio recording system is that the original recording remains unchanged. The final edited soundtrack is re-generated anew from the same files every time a new mix is produced. This means that the final mix can be altered at any time – even after its 'completion'. Disc recording systems are used in workstations.

Workstations

Workstations are complete audio post-production systems, often allowing sound to be entirely edited and mixed within the digital domain. Instead of a synchronizing controller and console with many hundreds of knobs and tens of faders, access and manipulation of the audio can be via a keyboard and screen. A mouse (hand controller) provides a means of moving an indicating arrow (cursor) about the screen to access information. Some screens are touch sensitive.

A workstation audio post-production system must not only have sufficient capacity to be able to record all the necessary material needed for a programme, but must in addition, have fast processing power to allow the material to be quickly retrieved for editing. Facilities are improving all the time, and manufacturers regularly update equipment with new software. The basic control of the system comes from the hardware, which can also be updated.

Such ˙ ˙ the quality of digital disc recording, that it should no longer be necessary to choose between recording systems on the basis of technical quality. Other factors, now come into play, such as 'user friendliness', capacity and speed of access.

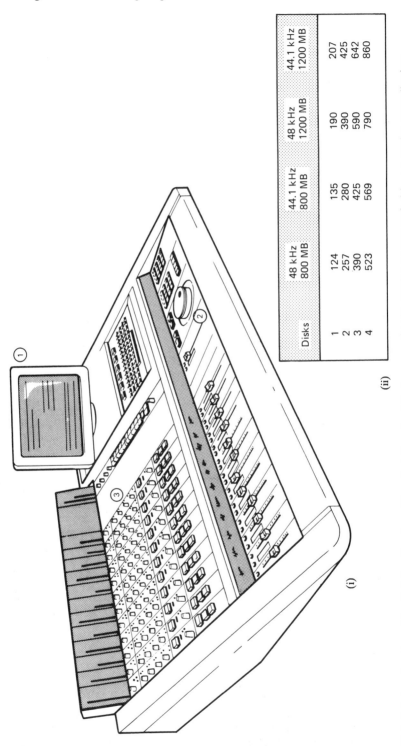

(i)

(ii)

Disks	48 kHz 800 MB	44.1 kHz 800 MB	48 kHz 1200 MB	44.1 kHz 1200 MB
1	124	135	190	207
2	257	280	390	425
3	390	425	590	642
4	523	569	790	860

(i) A digital workstation with a digital audio mixer; (1) work station visual display screen (see illustration on page 116); (2) work station controller (see illustration on page 63); (3) input channel (see illustration on page 147); (ii) Track minutes of storage time available on 800 and 1200 megabyte recording discs

Compact discs

The digital compact disc found in the home was developed from video disc technology and is widely used in audio post-production. Compact discs are marked with three letters to indicate the recording path.

DDD	Digital tape recorder used during original recording session mixing and/or editing and transcription mastering
ADD	Analogue tape recorder used during original recording session digital tape recorder used during mixing and/or editing and transcription mastering
AAD	Analogue tape recorder used during original recording session and mixing and/or editing, digital tape recorder used in transcription mastering

The markings used on compact discs detailing the recording path

Their instant access, immunity to handling problems and superb quality make them ideal as a storage medium for sound effects and music libraries. They are also produced to an international standard.

Like the conventional long playing vinyl record, the compact disc has a spiral track on its surface – but the track starts at the inside of the disc and works outwards. The disc is 120 mm in diameter and has about 2000 information spirals in the programme area. The actual recording takes the form of a series of laser cut indentations (pits) of eight different lengths. They are tied to a tracking speed of 1.2 metres per second, the rotational speed of the disc varying from 200–500 rpm to maintain a true linear speed. The digital data is recorded at a sampling rate of 44.1 kHz, with 16 bit resolution per channel for the left and right channels.

The compact disc offers a higher recording capacity than any form of analogue recording system, and has the additional advantage of there being no physical contact, and therefore no wear, between the head and the medium.

The compact disc cannot be erased or re-recorded and is, therefore, in computer terms a write once, read many times, or 'WORM' device. A further set of letters DRAW describes the generation of discs that can record and play back without processing (Direct read after write). These discs find particular use in workstations for storing sound effects, and they can be removed from the systems for exchange unlike hard discs.

Magnetic tape

Audio magnetic tape has an excellent storage capacity, a large area of sound in terms of tracks, and can be rolled up into a small space. Access, however, is only possible by spooling through the tapes – this can be slow. It is impossible to gain access to the end of a tape without unrolling the material up to that point. Data discs, on the other hand, have their surface

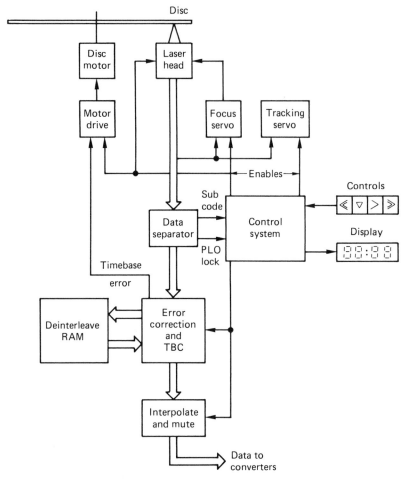

A CD player schematic showing audio and control servo paths (*From J. Watkinson, The Art of Digital Audio, by permission*)

permanently accessible. Digital recording on reel to reel tapes is available in the Pro Digi, Dash, S Dat and R Dat formats. However, the systems are somewhat inconvenient in audio post-production, compared to their instant access, disc recording based counterparts.

The open reel stationary head digital audio recorder was introduced in the mid 1980s to replace the analogue recorder in the music recording studio. In the multitrack studio the mixing console was far out performing the tape recording system. In order to increase studio quality dramatically, it was merely necessary to replace the analogue tape recorder with a digital one. The Dash and Pro Digi format, reel to reel, digital recorders which were introduced, perform all the normal functions expected of an analogue multitrack recorder. They record sound by a system of multitrack heads, splitting data into various different channels.

Unfortunately, digital recording and open-reel transports are not really compatible. The short wavelengths required for digital recording rely on intimate head contact, and are very intolerant to tape contamination. To reduce contamination problems, rotating head digital audio format (RDat) and some stationary head formats, (SDat) use tape cassettes. These are small machines particularly suitable for location recording.

R-Dat

The R-Dat recording system records digital information at a high speed by using rotating heads. The track spacing can be very close because of this, allowing two hours of recording time at a sample rate of 44 kHz. The domestic versions sample at 48 kHz. Much of the technology for the recording system has been developed from the compact disc.

A tape width of 3.8 mm is used, matching that of an ordinary compact cassette, although the cassette itself is slightly smaller. The tape is scanned by two record/replay heads, giving a 90 degree wrap around the drum. The small degree of wrap reduces tape wear and the likelihood of tape breakage. The head drum is rotated at a speed of 2000 revs per minute. A specific track provides information for automatic tracking to help maintain tape speed, as well as information on the number of channels and the sampling frequency. The normal tape speed is 8.150 mm per second, but there are additional speeds available with four sampling rates. The speed itself is very accurately controlled as in all digital audio recording devices, by quartz crystal.

Access with R-Dat is good. The tape speed is slow, therefore rewinding to a given section is quick. The drum is small and lock-up immediate. There is a certain degree of user information that can be recorded on the machine, and cues can be inserted so the player will skip from one point to another for editing and quick retrieval. This facility is not designed, however, for great accuracy and it is not entirely suitable for time code information. The low linear speed of the cassette means that the longitudinal tracks of the R-Dat format are unusable for time code. However, certain manufactuers produce accurate time code interfaces and these machines provide an excellent substitute for quarter-inch time code tape recorders, in the field.

Pulse code modulation recording

The PCM audio recording system is used to record digital sound onto videotape recorders. Despite being the earliest digital audio recording system developed, it still finds use today. To record digital audio onto a videotape recorder is not easy – audio signals are continuous and video signals are intermittent. However, a high writing speed is available from a videotape recorder.

Each frame of a video picture is made up of two fields or two vertical scans produced by an electron gun which creates a set of lines across the television screen. There is a time gap between these fields, known as the

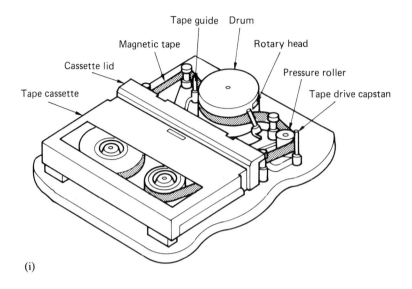

(i)

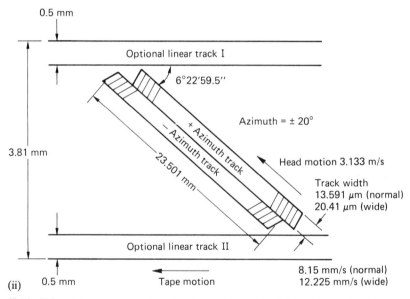

(i) The R Dat recording mechanism; (ii) The R Dat head track layout (*From J. Watkinson, The Art of Digital Audio, by permission*)

field synchronization period, when recordings cannot be made. By 'compressing time' it is possible to fit the audio signal into this intermittent video signal. The recording does not take place in real time but is compressed and expanded, so covering the time gap. As information comes out of the RAM memory it immediately releases more space for information to be placed in it.

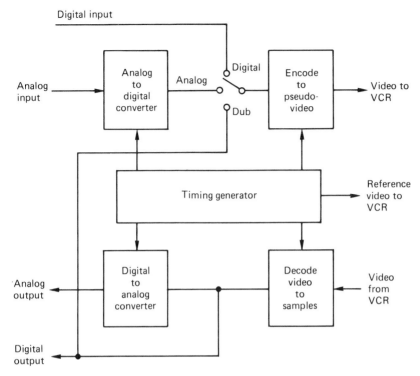

The PCM recording system including a connection to allow copying for editing purposes
(*From J. Watkinson, The Art of Digital Audio, by permission*)

A selection of sampling rates are available with PCM systems, thereby determining the frequency response of the systems.
Digital sound is:

1. Expensive in its professional formats.
2. Of almost perfect quality.
3. Available cheaply in domestic formats.
4. Good for access.
5. Subject to very unacceptable distortion if it reaches any overload point.
6. Subject to slow run-up times in decoding the sound if the system processors are fully loaded.
7. Without residual level after erasure.
8. Without print through.
9. Without a universal format.
10. Often unable to be checked in playback while recording, to ensure that the recording is present.
11. Able to run at a locked reference speed.

Recording audio for post-production

Up to now we have examined the equipment and the electronic control systems used in the audio post-production studio. This chapter examines the processes leading up to the final recording of the soundtrack.

Film and video soundtracks can be reproduced successfully in any type of environment but their accompanying pictures cannot. Generally, film is most suitable for theatrical releases; television, on the other hand, is more suitable for distribution to individual homes, where many small groups of people can watch the smaller screen. The large size of the projected motion picture image, compared with the electronic television screen, means that films tend to be more precisely made, since technical and artistic finishes are far more easily seen.

The production techniques used in the making of motion picture films and electronic television programmes are traditionally very different, although it is possible to integrate the two by taking advantage of the best of both systems. For example, in commercials for television it is not unusual to use 35 mm film on location, maintaining the highest resolution and contrast ratios, and then transfer the original negative to videotape for sophisticated special effects manipulation. However, to work successfully these techniques rely on expensive and sophisticated systems. Most studio or location 'shoots' use simple, conventional, tried and tested methods.

Multiple camera videotape recording

Originally, broadcast television pictures could not be recorded or edited, and all productions were transmitted live. Two or more cameras would simultaneously shoot a scene and the various outputs were cut together as the programme was transmitted. The sound was transmitted 'live', as it happened.

In a studio production, the audio supervisor is responsible for the recorded sound balance. He mixes together the various sound sources, and may be assisted by an operator who controls pre-recorded sounds from cartridge machines, tape recorders and disc players. To assist the sound mixer on the studio floor, there may be a 'boom swinger' operating a microphone on an extending arm. The sound mixer sitting in the control

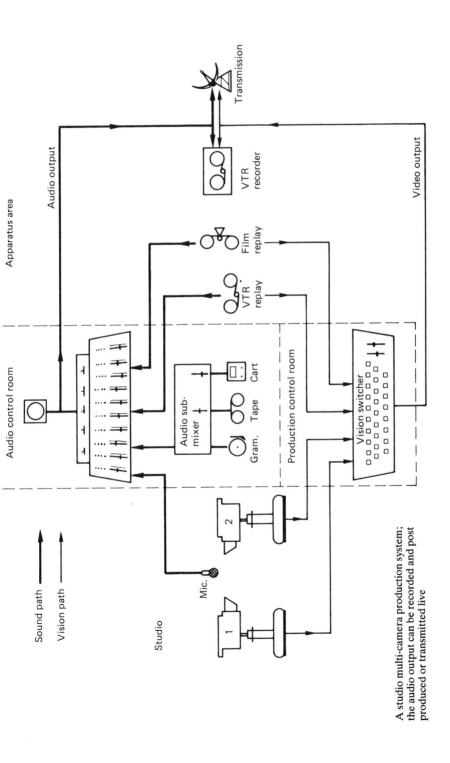

A studio multi-camera production system; the audio output can be recorded and post produced or transmitted live

room, listens to the output of the boom and his other sources and balances them together. Since the boom microphone has to cover all the action as it progresses on the studio floor, the microphone sound pick-up needs to be wide, and may sound over 'bright'. This can be extenuated by the height of the sets, designed to allow lights in, and the bare floors which are necessary to allow cameras to track over them. The sound mixer will compensate for this through his mixing console and the facilities it offers.

If the sound mixer knows that the programme he is working on is to be recorded and audio post-produced, he may decide to leave the process of modifying, and adding additional sounds, until later; well away from the tensions in the control room.

Single camera shooting (video and film)

Single camera productions are shot in a discontinuous manner, with one camera shooting all the material needed. The action is recorded; the camera stopped and moved; the lights changed to their best position; then the action continues. In editing, the various shots are then cut together to make a complete sequence. The sound is recorded at the same time as the picture, but it is often incomplete. Single camera recording may take place away from the studio and sound control room. Often the sound recordist has only his headphones and experience to monitor the quality of the sound, so he tries to produce the best possible quality sound from what is, quite frequently, the most unsuitable locations. To produce the 'cleanest' sound he may, if he knows there is audio post-production time available, record separately each sound that makes up a scene.

A simple scene may, for example, consist of two people walking, talking to each other and then driving away in separate cars. The scene will consist of many separate sounds – the feet of the two characters meeting; the talk between the two, consisting of a separate recording of each; the doors slamming and the noise of the two cars starting. In addition, the general background noise of the complete scene is needed. This may be cars going by, birds singing, street vendors or activity in a harbour. The sound scene is more than just one picture following another, it consists of sounds that geographically, and in time, knit together the whole discontinuous scene. The amount of post-production time available will influence the sound recordist on his approach to the job. The more time that there is available for audio post-production, the more additional material he can record, and the 'cleaner' the various recordings will be. It may even be an advantage to record more than one track of sound during a take.

Single camera recording with multitrack separate sound

There are certain advantages of recording sound on more than just one track of the recorder whether in a studio or on location. If a scene consists of various sounds all happening at the same time, these can each be recorded separately onto the tracks of a multitrack tape recorder, and later mixed in audio post-production at the appropriate levels required.

On-screen lines can be recorded on one track and off-screen lines on another, or, if artistes are fitted with their own personal, miniature neck microphones each can be recorded onto a separate track, as the action takes place. This allows considerable flexibility in post-production, although much depends on the time available. Even a two track recorder can be used to advantage, particularly when two artistes are speaking with very different microphone sound quality. For example, one may be recorded with a personal microphone under many layers of clothing, producing a muffled sound, the other with a personal microphone which is hardly hidden. These two, very different, sounds can be recorded on separate tracks of the tape recorder, and later 'sweetened' in audio post-production, where the sound quality can be judged critically. Similarly, action which can only be recorded once, such as an explosion, can be recorded in close-up on one track, and in a long shot on another.

Music is often recorded on location using a multitrack tape recorder. Here, individual instruments, or groups of instruments, can be recorded onto the various tracks of the recorder for mixing later, in a music studio. Normally, a rough mix from various tracks is provided at the time of the recording. This is transferred onto a synchronous sprocketed film or videotape for use as a guide track in editing. While the editing takes place the music is mixed in a specialized music recording studio.

Slating

When using film cameras, the sound and picture are recorded separately. This is called double system shooting. To match both of these together for editing later, it is normal to provide a synchronous mark on the soundtrack and on the picture. (The two machines only run together in synchronization, at speed). The accepted way of doing this is by using a clapper-board. Before the Director starts the action he asks the sound recordist to 'turn over sound' then the cameraman to 'turn the camera'. When both the camera and the recorder are running at the synchronous speed, the Director calls 'mark' and a board, on which is written the scene and take numbers is shot visually, and then a hinged clapper is closed on the top, making an audible signal. Later, these two can be conformed into synchronization or 'sunk up'. The numbers on the board provide information as to the slate (the shot number), and the take (the number of times it has been filmed). These techniques are also used for videotaping. It is unnecessary here to use the clapper; however, the slate and take numbers are still relevant, providing quick visual information with the time code being referred to them. Separately recorded sound effects and dialogue are also identified as individual slates.

In the video production the sound will be recorded onto the videotape carrying the pictures or, possibly, onto a separate tape recorder, which is again synchronized with the video camera. In this situation time code from the video camera will be recorded onto an audio tape recorder providing synchronizing information. The sound may also be recorded both onto the videotape recorder, as well as onto the separate audio tape recorder. The sound on the videotape recorder will then provide a guide track to the video editor who does not need to work with a separate sound machine. Time code provides the necessary information to enable the separate sound and picture to be synchronized later.

Double system or single system?

Modern video recorders are able to record sound using audio frequency modulation (AFM) and pulse code modulation (PCM) techniques to a very high standard, and arguments that separate sound systems produce better audio quality are only now valid in film situations. Here separate sound is the norm, since combined magnetic sound film recording is unacceptable, both from an operational and a quality point of view. The automatic synchronizing of separate sound and picture is called auto-conforming.

Recording sound with a sound machine independent of the camera, with no lead between the two, has certain operational advantages.

1. In certain situations it is physically safer to record sound without an interconnecting lead – such as on small boats or on scaffolding, where extra cabling may prove dangerous.
2. Without lead restrictions the camera, recorder and microphones can be easily placed wherever required.
3. Complete sound recordings of current affairs events are possible without breaks. Film cameras and video cameras used in these situations often have a limited recording time.
4. The sound recordist can record sound whenever he wishes, without needing access to the camera; these sounds may be wildtracks, sound only interviews, etc.
5. With multi-camera video shoots using cam-corders (a video camera and recorder combined), it is often difficult for the sound recordist to feed his audio signal separately to two or more roving cameras; separate sound here, provides a master soundtrack.

Picture film gauge (mm)	Method of providing sound	Code name
35	Combined optical track	35 comopt
35	Combined magnetic track	35 commag
16	Combined optical track	16 comopt
16	Combined magnetic track	16 commag
35	Optical track on separate 35-mm film	35 sepopt
35	Magnetic track on separate 35-mm film	35 sepmag
16	Optical track on separate 16-mm film	16 sepopt
16	Magnetic track on separate 16-mm film	16 sepmag
35	Picture only	35 mute
16	Picture only	16 mute

Various combined and separate film sound formats for 35 mm and 16 mm film

Multi-camera film shooting

Film cameras can be used in multi-camera set-ups, similar to video set-ups in, for example the recording of 'Music Concerts'. No attempt is made to produce an edited master, as would happen in a video studio. While shooting, each camera may be run continuously or as required. For these purposes special time code systems have been developed. These allow any number of cameras to be started or stopped during a shoot, without any traditional, synchronizing clapper boards being used. After the shoot, the code recorded onto the location audio tape is transferred, with the sound, onto sprocketed magnetic film. The code is also printed on the back of the film, in legible numbers. The pictures are also recorded with code, and the two can be easily synchronized. If this system is unavailable, time code can be used equally successfully but in a rather less sophisticated way in multi-camera filming. Each camera is crystal quartz controlled to a precise speed. The start of each shot is identified with a time code figure, recorded by photographing a jumbo-size, displayed time code reader. This is fed from the output of the crystal controlled master generator which also synchronizes the audio recorder. The display is centrally placed so that all the cameras can see it. Each time a camera is run, the display is filmed and this record of the time code provides a reference for the editor in 'syncing up'. He matches the picture to the sound which has been transferred to sprocketed magnetic film, with time code printed on the back.

Time code generators and cameras

Where a time code generator is fitted as extra 'outboard' equipment to an existing video recorder, it is important to ensure that the time code is synchronized to the video pictures, so that each code word begins at a specific point in the field blanking interval, otherwise the code may be unusable in editing.

Time code generators used in conjunction with camera equipment on location can be set in two separate ways, record run and free run, both can affect audio post-production operations.

Record run

In record run, the time generator is set at the beginning of the day, or alternatively, at the beginning of each tape and can be used as an accurate timer of tape length. The code generator only runs when the video or audio tape machine is recording, thus the time code recorded on the tape is, when played back, both continuous and consecutive. This can be important if the audio post-production synchronizer used, can only successfully read a stream of consecutive time code. Synchronizers, for example, using tachometer pulses at high speed are confused if time code is not consecutive and are not designed to work discontinuous code.

Free run

Time code in free run mode produces discontinuous code. In the free run mode the time code generator is set to the real time of day using an accurate clock. It is started and left to run like a clock, continuously. Other equipment, such as a second camera, or an audio tape recorder, may well be synchronized to the same time code. However, each of these time code generators may not be sufficiently accurate to hold synchronization over many hours. There can be problems, particularly with some video recorders, if, for example, the heater is switched on or the batteries are changed and it is advisable to carry out an accuracy test to check the reliability of equipment. Syncing-up material with inaccurate time code can cause immense problems in audio post-production. Alternatively, time code can be radioed to the various recording devices from a central generator.

In free run the time code generator acts as an accurate stop watch, timing events as they happen, irrespective of whether the recorders are on or off.

This is useful for current affairs programming, such as conferences or sports matches, where it is important to know when selected events happened. Since the time code is tied to the real time of day, notes can be made from a digital wristwatch without access to the camera. Using time of day allows everyone to make their own time code notes, without physically examining the camera's time code position.

Recording dialogue at time of shooting

It is the responsibility of the sound mixer to record the best possible sound he can, even under the most difficult conditions. Sound effects can be recreated in audio post-production, but dialogue is far more costly and difficult to re-record satisfactorily. Therefore, the sound recordist should primarily concentrate on producing high quality dialogue recordings.

The well recorded dialogue track will consist of only those sounds that the sound mixer wishes to record. He will decide on the 'fullness' of the tracks by taking into account the audio post-production time and facilities available. The ideal dialogue track for audio post-production will:

1. be recorded without reverberation. Reverberation cannot be taken out of a recording but it can easily be added. (In stereo, reverberation may be part of the sound field).
2. be recorded with only one artiste speaking at a time. Speech should only overlap for good reasons – such as an argument.
3. be consistent in level, quality and stereo position between takes. This means fewer changes have to be made in audio post-production, which can be time consuming.
4. not be recorded too wide if stereo is used.

If it is impossible to record dialogue successfully because of poor acoustics or high background noise, the sound recordist may decide to record the dialogue again. This will usually be done after the original take, as a track for 'fitting', without the camera running, using a more controlled location, or just 'closer' sound. The editor will then attempt to fit this against the original dialogue. It is obviously important that the actors record the dialogue with the same intonation and at the same speed. They must also use the same words, often actors unwittingly use different words for different takes, and this can make 'fitting' particularly difficult!

Once the dialogue has been shot the numerous other sounds needed for audio post-production will be recorded, such as spot effects and wild tracks.

Spot effects

Spot effects are often added in audio post-production from the location tapes. Keys being turned in a car door, for example, might be recorded separately as a spot effect on location, and added during post-production rather than being recorded as part of a dialogue sequence. While dialogue is being spoken the key effect may be of a very low level and masked, for example, by the background noise of cars going by. If added in post-production, the key effect can be increased in volume to the level required. Spot effects benefit from being recorded separately from the main track.

Wild tracks

Wild tracks, or atmospheric recordings, are background recordings to scenes. They provide the atmosphere of a location and are 'wild' or non-synchronous. Wild tracks are also used to help cover the problems of variations in background level between edited shots. When dialogue is recorded discontinuously, the background level between shots is likely to vary. The dialogue levels will be the same, but as the picture cuts the background sound levels may change suddenly and unacceptably. An 'atmos' track can be added to mask this 'stepping' effect if it is played at the level of the shot with the highest background noise.

Recording effects separately on location is particularly important when moving objects which produce their own sounds, such as cars, are used in productions. Very often synchronous recordings of cars are incomplete and so extra wildtracks have to be recorded. These wild tracks should consist, for example of various shots of the car coming in and out of vision, the door opening and closing, the engine starting, ticking over, revving, stopping, pulling away and changing gear, together with interior shots of it running.

Identification

All sound recorded on location must be well identified for retrieval. Each tape, video or sound, should be identified with the date, the production name and number, the tape number and details of the tracks recorded on it. If they were close-ups, long shots, rehearsals, wild tracks, etc. with time code systems, the time is also logged as the sound is recorded.

Shooting to playback

This is a technique used in musical productions, where discontinuous single camera shooting is used. A musical number will often consist of various shots at different angles, allowing the camera a great deal of freedom. To cover these shots successfully with microphones and record quality sound is almost impossible, since the microphones would have to be positioned for the widest shot used. So rather than record 'live', the sound is recorded in a studio under controlled conditions, or even at the location, using the best possible microphone positions. It is then played back to the artistes, who mime while the camera roams unhindered; stopping and starting whenever the director requires. In a well organized shoot the director will know precisely how to shoot each section of music. Tapes can then be prepared against a shooting script. In film making, to assist editing, three beeps of sound are recorded on the tape prior to the particular audio take. This allows the camera assistant to mime the last beep, with a clapperboard in front of the camera. In this situation the playback tape recorder and the video or film camera are synchronized together, possibly locked to one central, external generator, or each running under its own crystal oscillator.

Other methods can be used:

1. A playback tape recorder sends audio simultaneously to the location or set and into a second recorder which re-records playback sound synchronized signals, to the camera. The material is edited in the normal way, using the re-recorded sound.
2. The playback audio machine runs in synchronization with the camera, using time code. This time code is also fed to an audio track of the video recorder. Using separate sound editing, the pictures are then automatically locked-up to their appropriate, separate playback tape through the time code.

Whatever system is used, identification and filing have to be carefully considered. When the shooting is completed the original music tape may well be re-mixed during the final re-recording session.

9

Video editing picture and sound

To understand the processes of audio post-production, it is necessary to be aware of not only how material is recorded on location, but also how the pictures are edited. Different techniques are used for different types of programme material. This depends on whether a production is photographed on film or recorded on video, and whether a single camera or multi-camera technique is used.

The video editing suite in its simplest from consists of two video machines, one a player and the other a picture recorder, with a controller. As the suite becomes more complicated other equipment, such as a caption generator, another video player, and vision mixer, are added. In video editing, the picture and sound are copied rather than physically being cut, as happens in film.

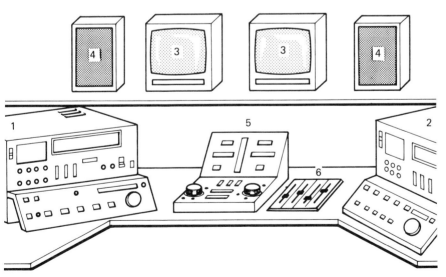

A simple editing suite; 1, cassette player for camera masters; 2, recorder for editing onto; 3, monitors to view pictures on; 4, loudspeakers; 5, audio mixer for controlling the sound tracks

Originally, video editing systems used the picture control synchronizing track of the videotape recorder to control the editing process. This track is in the form of electronic pulses, recorded along the edge of the tape. In a similar way to film sprockets, these can be set to zero on a time counter. They can then be used to control the video editing process. However, these pulses cannot be read accurately like film sprockets, and were superseded by time code which provides frame to frame editing accuracy.

Videotape editing is carried out by copying pictures from a replay machine onto a recorder. Two specific methods are used, assembly editing and insert editing. In the assembly edit mode pictures are added to already existing recordings, each picture is complete with its own time code (recorded at the shoot), and the synchronizing control pulses needed to produce steady pictures. However, when another picture is added to a previous one, the control track pulses are now discontinuous. Each time the picture cuts, the synchronous control information changes. This is likely to produce unstable pictures at the cut and the soundtrack may well 'wow'.

In the insert mode the control pulses are continuous, so there is no disturbance of the edit. However, to achieve this, the tape has to be prepared for an editing session by pre-striping with continuous control track and time code (blacking). The pictures recorded onto the tape are locked to the pre-striped track, and there are no frame rolls on cuts.

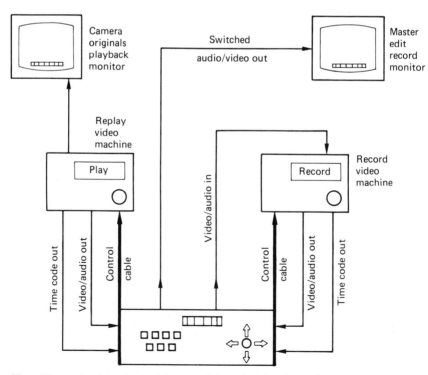

The editing system for a simple videotape editing suite using time code

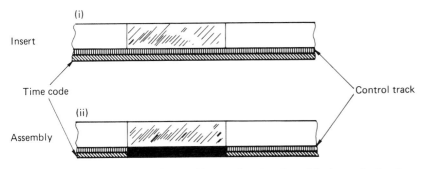

(i)

Insert

Time code   Control track

(ii)

Assembly

(i) Insert editing uses a pre-striped tape with control track and possibly time code already recorded on it. This track remains undisturbed during editing; (ii) Assembly editing adds a new control track with each picture edit.

However, the time code on the original camera masters does not appear on the edited videotape.

A video edit progresses as the picture is dubbed, from the playback machine, onto the recording machine. The machines are controlled from an edit controller which may include a computer keyboard and a video display screen. Shots are chosen visually as in film editing, but they can be found by giving the player time code location addresses. Having selected the edit, the necessary time code readings are entered and the edit computer then rehearses the sequence. Once the complete edit rehearsal, or preview, has been performed successfully, the system goes into record. Each of these edits may be memorized on a small computer disc which can

			Title: Sample Edit List			
			Customer name here			
V A1 A2						00:06:58:17
			In	Out	Duration	Time-code
	Mstr		01:06:23:11			/PLA N-01:17:06:05
Dissolve						
C to A 060	A-077		12:10:37:20	12:10:44:04	00:00:06:14	/Cue N-12:10:34:00
	B-0 05		12:35:18:28	12:35:18:28		/STP N-12:35:19:08
Autotrim	C-084		12:39:18:24	12:39:18:24		/LOS D-12:42:06:20
Sort rec-in	AUX					REC OFF DISK ON
Event #020	Black					CO N-13:31:25:14
A mode assembly, events:						

014	084	A1/V	C		12:39:13:20	12:39:18:24	01:06:18:07	01:06:23:11
015	081	AA	C		12:35:01:06	12:35:18:28	01:06:23:11	01:06:41:03
> 016	084	V	C		12:39:18:24	12:39:18:24	01:06:23:11	01:06:23:11 <
> 016	077	V	D	060	13:10:37:20	13:10:44:04	01:06:23:11	01:06:29:25 <
017	077	V	C		13:26:17:02	13:26:22:02	01:06:29:25	01:06:34:25
017	084	V	W019	045	12:35:04:03	12:35:10:11	01:06:34:25	01:06:41:03
018	081	AA/V	C		12:37:08:02	12:37:11:02	01:06:41:03	01:06:44:03
018	081	AA/V	K B		12:37:11:02	12:37:18:23	01:05:44:03	01:06:51:24
018	AX	AA/V	K	030	00:00:00:00	00:00:06:21	01:06:44:03	01:06:50:24
019	077	A2/V	K B	(F)	12:19:37:19	12:19:44:12	01:06:51:24	01:00:58:17
019	084	A2/V	K 0	090	12:53:00:19	12:53:04:12	01:06:51:24	01:06:55:17

1-

2-

3-

A CMX edit decision list 1, menu area; 2, system message area; 3, edit decision list (*Courtesy of F W O Bauch Limited*)

produce a print-out in the form of an edit decision list (EDL). This tends to be in a standard format, showing the tape source, the edit In point, edit Out point, video reel number and the edit duration.

In film editing, pictures are physically cut together. As the picture edit progressed, the sound is cut at the same time onto a separate roll of sound film (any relevant sound not used being filed away for later track laying). In video editing, however, some or all of the soundtrack laying takes place during the picture edit. Videotape formats have available, up to four tracks of sound, and these can be used to good effect by the video editor as the picture edit progresses. Unfortunately though, in some formats two of these tracks are audio frequency modulation tracks, and have limited use since audio recordings can only be made when video recording takes place.

Well laid soundtracks can save much time in the audio post production suite. In particular care should be taken as to which of the video recorder's audio tracks the edited sound should be sent to. It is important that the sound should move to an alternative track (off laid) when the incoming signal:

1. Requires audio equalization changes.
2. Has a disturbing increase in background level on a cut.
3. Changes scene.
4. Has a high level of incoming or outgoing sound against a previous or following low level sound.
5. Requires special effects such as reverberation etc.

The facilities offered in many video editing suites allow audio changes like these to be carried out during video editing.

Discontinuous shooting can create particular problems in video editing when only a limited number of soundtracks are available on the video recorder.

Example of video sound editing with discontinuous shooting

In a restaurant scene for an example, additional sounds may well be required to augment synchronous dialogue. These might include sound effects such as a cup being put down, a door being opened and closed or a waitress walking in and dropping a tray of crockery. Should the waitress walk off-screen talking, while other characters carry on with their speeches, the waitress will need to be laid on track 2 and the featured dialogue will carry on, on track 1.

Should a firebell go off during the restaurant scene and be shown in close-up, the videotape editor will have insufficient tracks. He will, therefore, have to leave this effect off, making a note on the edit decision list of the time code of the original recording, and the number of the appropriate tape. The sound of the bell will then be added later, in the audio post-production suite. These effects can then be 'laid in' directly from the original master videotape, which may have been transferred onto a separate appropriate synchronous audio format.

Other sounds may also need to be laid in later because of limited track space. These will include the 'sound heads' and 'tails' of shots; that is the early and late parts of shots that were discarded in the picture edit, but include important sounds. For example, in a scene where a car is passing, that car may only be seen for a few seconds but to complete the scene it must be heard for much longer – i.e. as it enters and leaves the scene. Therefore sound heads and tails are added to the edited picture shot. Sounds which continue before or after a picture edit are called split edits. This technique cannot be used when sound is recorded 'in vision' using audio frequency modulation recording.

It is important that any additional sounds that are required from the master camera originals are well logged at the video editing stage.

Audio editing problems in the video editing suite can be eased somewhat, if the more expensive continuous shooting system is used with full vision and sound mixing facilities. In this situation some of the needs for audio post-production can be eliminated, because the sound mixer will have sufficient facilities to produce a more complete soundtrack which requires less sound editing. In the restaurant scene, for example, each sequence might be shot continuously using two cameras. The mixed sound would then include all the voices recorded onto track 1 of the edited videotape, allowing the single shot of the firebell to be dropped in at the appropriate point on track 2. Some additional sounds would be added in audio post-production, perhaps the clink of cups, featured footsteps, background music etc.

Editing separate sound with video

It is possible for a video production to be shot with separate sound, using time code to synchronize together the camera and the separate audio recorder (which will probably be a multitrack tape machine). In this case, the soundtrack will need to be synchronized with its appropriate picture during editing. Alternatively, a sound guide track is recorded on the videotape recorder in the field, for use in the editing suite. Later, the master soundtrack is synchronized to the edited master in audio post-production. This is relatively simple if the original location time code has been preserved on the edited picture copy, either in the form of a second time code track, or in the form of an edit decision list. Ideally the EDL will calculate and provide the information for the time code off-set which is required between the edited pre-striped videotape, with continuous time code, and the separate original audio tapes with camera time code.

This type of separate sound system tends to be used in special situations where a separate sound recorder to the camera is essential, as in musical programmes requiring multitrack recording techniques.

It is possible to stay in the separate sound format throughout the videotape editing process. Here the videotape player that holds the master camera original is locked to an audio tape player of the same format as used in the field – perhaps a centre time code machine. Since both the audio tape and the videotape recorded in the field have the same time code, they stay in synchronization. The edit is assembled onto a video recorder that also has a time coded audio tape recorder following it. As the picture edit progresses, the audio from the playback audio machine is transferred onto the edit audio recorder. The sound follows and conforms directly, in separate sound, throughout the edit.

In this situation, when audio tape recorders are used in video edit suites to chase video machines, it is convenient if the audio machine is considered by the video controller as a videotape recorder. The audio transport can then be dropped in and out of record and wound forward or backwards to the commands of the video edit keyboard – as though it were one of the video machines.

In a video editing suite soundtracks can also be laid directly onto a separate videotape, which are copies of the edited master tape with time code. In this method it is possible to build up any number of tracks using multiple tapes. (The high cost of video editing suites means that this may be an uneconomic way of laying soundtracks). These sound 'video' tapes are then played off in synchronization and mixed within the edit suite or alternatively, dumped onto a multitrack tape recorder where they are mixed in a sound suite. As a rule, it can be generally said that laying many soundtracks in a video editing suite is uneconomic.

Off-line editing

Editing video pictures using camera master original tapes throughout, from preview through to editing, is called on-line editing. The complete equipment used, including high quality video recorders, vision mixers, graphic design equipment, colour correction equipment etc., is expensive in terms of hire charges or capital outlay.

To reduce cost, a separate approach has been developed where the master material is copied onto low quality video cassettes with burnt-in time code. Editing decisions are made, using this low cost format. This is called off-line editing.

Off-line facilities vary in their degree of sophistication, and special provisions have to be made on these low cost formats for frame-accurate editing. In the EBU system, a band width of 2.7 mHz is necessary to record vertical internal time code for frame-accurate editing. This is not readily achieved in the standard domestic VHS/Betamax format used for off-line editing and special pre-striping techniques are used. Alternatively, less accurate longitudinal time code can be used on an audio track. U-matic industrial machines are capable of accurate editing, but are more expensive than domestic cassette recorders.

The simplest form of off-line editing is just a single VHS or Beta format machine used to view and select scenes. This usually entails the use of a time code reader, to burn time code readings in the form of visual numbers into the picture of the off-line copy. These are used to form a list of editing points for the start and finish of the frames of each scene. These provide the reference for the on-line editor to assemble the camera originals.

In more sophisticated systems, editing actually takes place using a two machine suite. These are capable of editing to the exact frame. However, dissolves and special effects are not possible, and notes have to be made of these requirements. The resultant off-line edit carries with it in VITC, the

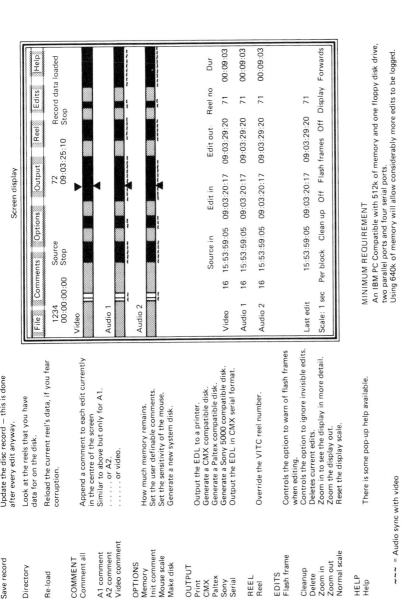

Screen display

File	Comments	Options	Output	Reel	Edits	Help
1234 00:00:00:00	Source Stop		72 09:03:25:10		Record data loaded Stop	

Video

Audio 1

Audio 2

		Source in	Edit in	Edit out	Reel no	Dur
Video	16	15:53:59:05	09:03:20:17	09:03:29:20	71	00:09:03
Audio 1	16	15:53:59:05	09:03:20:17	09:03:29:20	71	00:09:03
Audio 2	16	15:53:59:05	09:03:20:17	09:03:29:20	71	00:09:03
Last edit		15:53:59:05	09:03:20:17	09:03:29:20	71	
Scale: 1 sec	Per block	Clean up Off	Flash frames Off	Display Forwards		

MINIMUM REQUIREMENT
An IBM PC Compatible with 512k of memory and one floppy disk drive, two parallel ports and four serial ports.
Using 640k of memory will allow considerably more edits to be logged.

Save record — Update the disc record – this is done after every edit anyway.

Directory — Look at the reels that you have data for on the disk.

Re-load — Reload the current reel's data, if you fear corruption.

COMMENT
Comment all — Append a comment to each edit currently in the centre of the screen
A1 comment — Similar to above but only for A1.
A2 comment — ...... or A2.
Video comment — ...... or video.

OPTIONS
Memory — How much memory remains.
Init comment — Set the user definable comments.
Mouse scale — Set the sensitivity of the mouse.
Make disk — Generate a new system disk.

OUTPUT
Print — Output the EDL to a printer.
CMX — Generate a CMX compatible disk.
Paltex — Generate a Paltex compatible disk.
Sony — Generate a Sony 5000 compatible disk.
Serial — Output the EDL in CMX serial format.

REEL
Reel — Override the VITC reel number.

EDITS
Flash frame — Controls the option to warn of flash frames when editing.
Cleanup — Controls the option to ignore invisible edits.
Delete — Deletes current edits.
Zoom in — Zoom in to see the display in more detail.
Zoom out — Zoom the display out.
Normal scale — Reset the display scale.

HELP
Help — There is some pop-up help available.

~~ = Audio sync with video

An off line editing menu showing video and two audio tracks, displayed as part of a frame accurate VHS off line editing system (JVC) (*Courtesy of JVC Professional Products (UK) Ltd*)

actual time codes from the camera originals, making automatic conforming possible. In this simple form of off-line editing the sound and picture are cut together. However, if the sound edits are separate from picture edits (split edits), or the sound is sourced from a different camera tape, this simple off-line editing suite is unsuitable. It is then necessary to store the sound editing time code information separately from the picture editing information. To record this information, a computer is provided with a floppy disc drive. A video display unit graphically displays the video and soundtracks as they are edited and laid, with the floppy disc providing an editing decision list for both video and sound.

The more facilities offered within the off-line editing suite, the more expensive the system becomes. Off-line sound editing can become complicated and it is often simpler to restrict off-line edits to video and two audio tracks only. These can easily be handled by the editor, specialist sound staff then deal with track-laying on-line.

Off laying sound and video in preparation for sound mixing

The videotape recorders used in off-line editing do not need to be of high quality, and are, therefore inexpensive. For these reasons such machines (usually U-matic format) are often used in audio post-production suites. The process of copying the video and sound from the edited master to the 'work' copy, for use in audio post-production, is called off-laying.

When video copies are made for use in the audio suite it is normal practice to record a copy of the time code in the picture area. The picture may even have 'burnt into' it, the time code of the original camera master. The time code provides information for cueing and searching, and will accurately display codes when the picture is in the still frame mode. The physical size of the time code information within the picture can be varied.

Alternatively, a production can be mixed to an edited master, using an expensive high quality video playback machine. However, there will obviously be no burnt-in code in the picture area. Time code can be injected into the picture from the recorder's time code track through a time code inserter, similar to the one used to produce burnt-in time code on dub copies. This inserter must be capable of reading time code at high speed, and will be slightly inaccurate at very low speeds if it is fed from a longitudinal time code track.

Whatever the type of video player used in the audio post-production suite, the sound has to be off-laid onto a multitrack tape recorder of between 2 and 24 tracks, allowing other sounds to be added synchronously before the final mix.

The off-lay can be controlled in various ways. The multitrack audio tape recorder can either be pre-striped with time code and then slaved to the time code off the video master, or the time code from the video master can be recorded directly onto the audio machine as the transfer takes place. Ideally the time code should be reshaped, rather than just duplicated. In this case no synchronizer is required, as the simultaneous recording of code on both formats guarantees synchronization between the picture and audio machine.

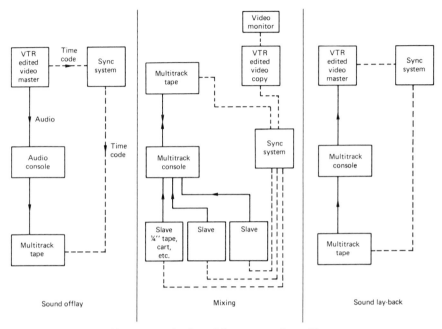

The multitrack audio video post-production mixing system using a video copy

The programme material now consists of a picture of reasonable quality, locked to an audio tape recorder which holds the high quality original sounds from the master edit. These soundtracks can now be prepared, ready for mixing and 'sweetening'.

10

Multitrack track laying

Certain equipment is required in the recording studio in order to lay soundtracks to video productions. Usually a multitrack tape recorder provides the main recording system. When locked by time code to a video player, it provides a method of storing sounds, in synchronization, ready for the mixing process. In order to play sounds onto the multitrack recorder a synchronous time coded tape recorder may be used together with cartridge machines, CD players, and vinyl disc players. A synchronizer controls the system, and a recording console sends the various sounds to the audio recorders.

Whatever type of audio post-production system is used – film, video or digital workstation – the basic steps to prepare the soundtrack are the same. First the picture is viewed and reviewed. The sound will consist of, perhaps synchronized dialogue, music that has been cut to picture, and some sound effects that were recorded synchronously on location. After the first viewing of the picture, notes are made about the sounds that will be needed for the final soundtrack, and the sounds that have already been laid onto the edited master.

The analysing of programmed material that has been edited is called track listing or spotting (USA). There are two different ways to spot a programme:

1. Starting at the top and working to the end, noting cues for all sounds required; dialogue, narration, music, effects, etc.
2. By noting only one particular type of sound or cue as the material is viewed, and repeating the process for each different type of sound, e.g. first viewing – dialogue cues, second viewing effects cues, etc.

Additional sounds needed will come from the original recordings made on location, from effects libraries, and music libraries. Some may come from recordings of dialogue, music or effects especially made for the production.

Time code	Video	Sound effect notes	Tracks							
			1	2	3	4	5	6	7	8
								Mix		Code
00:00	Edited master tracks		✕	✕						
00:00		Intro music/atmos			✕				✕	
00:00		C.· FX				✕				
00:11		Door open					✕			
00:14		Door close				✕				
00:30		Street vendor				✕				
00:44		Music out								
00:48										
⟶ 1:00		Footsteps			✕					
0:101		Keys in door					✕			
02:00		Engine start/idle			✕	✕				
02:10		Footsteps					✕			
02:30		Atmos cafe							✕	

An audio post-production spotting chart

Sound effects

Sound effects occur in any type of television or film production. Props are moved and make noises, doors open and close, actors move about as they perform, winds blow and waves crash on beaches. These effects give the soundtrack atmosphere; they reduce the pauses between dialogue lines and, hence, speed up the action.

Sound effects should not only be used because they obviously appear in picture, but also because they can become a valuable part of the sound picture. A distant train and hooter can, for example, add space to an open landscape. Every location has its own particular atmosphere. Even in a room with dead acoustic, the rustle of clothes can be heard, perhaps over the spot effects from a tea party. These can be added in the track laying process or during the final mix.

Many of the sound effects needed for a production will be provided by recordings from the location, some separately for 'fitting' in audio post-production, and some as part of the picture's soundtrack. Some of the effects will be chosen from a sound effects library.

Formats for sound effects

Sound effects libraries can be purchased complete in various forms, or alternatively effects can be purchased individually. Most audio post-production studios will hold their own effects library.

Long playing vinyl discs

Records were once a major source of sound effects material: they are easy to handle and have good access. More than thirty minutes of material can

CROSS SECTION
Chronological index

Track-index		Description	Time
X1	1-01	Cars and mopeds — southern European town/Greece	1:46
X1	2-01	Traffic queue — heavy traffic — cars and lorries	2:01
X1	3-01	Motor traffic — USA/Los Angeles — distant	1:31
X1	4-01	Fountain — in park	0:45
X1	5-01	Town Square — people and birds	1:42
X1	6-01	Road junction — squeaking brakes	1:30
X1	7-01	Rain — heavy — train station	1:04
X1	8-01	Vacuum cleaner	0:55
X1	9-01	Washing-up by hand	1:05
X1	10-01	Door creaking ver. 1 — large	0:15
X1	10-02	Door creaking ver. 2 — small	0:16
X1	11-01	Door-bell — ding-dong	0:07
X1	12-01	Knock on door — repeated twice	0:06
X1	13-01	Shower	0:36
X1	14-01	Fire in open fire-place	0:46
X1	15-01	Roller blind — up and down — flapping round	0:14
X1	16-01	Wall clock ticks — chimes 12	0:55
X1	17-01	Toilet flushing — old	0:21
X1	18-01	Tap running	0:18
X1	19-01	Alarm clock — mechanical — ticking	0:17
X1	20-01	Lambs — two, out of doors	0:58
X1	21-01	Brook — rushing	1:00
X1	22-01	Dogs barking — two — several together	0:15
X1	23-01	Cow — milking by hand	1:02
X1	24-01	Cows — in barn — restless	1:39
X1	25-01	Cows — in barn — contented	1:29
X1	26-01	Summer meadow — flies and birds	1:30
X1	27-01	Forest milieu — birds and a bumble bee	1:25
X1	28-01	Pig sty — lively	2:01
X1	29-01	Chicken clucking — rooster crowing	1:40
X1	30-01	Steam-train passing	1:06
X1	31-01	Car starts — and drives off — on gravel — Volvo	0:33
X1	32-01	Car passing — on gravel — 30 km/h	0:27
X1	33-01	Car arrives and stops — on gravel — handbrake	0:16
X1	34-01	Pick-up truck — Caterpillar — loading gravel	1:22
X1	35-01	Ferry — docking at quay — small	0:47
X1	36-01	Ship — engine — large	0:28
X1	37-01	Airplane — fighter — passing — Draken — 1180 km/h	0:43
X1	38-01	Helicopter — flying past — 4 Bell Augusta — distant	0:45
X1	39-01	Airplane — Jumbojet 747 — landing	0:53
X1	40-01	Airplane — Jumbojet 747 — taking off	0:39
X1	41-01	Train — Sub-way — Underground — stopping at platform	0:55
X1	42-01	Car hooter — compressor — 2 versions	0:07
X1	43-01	Electric drill	0:17
X1	44-01	Brewery — bottles rattling	1:32
X1	45-01	Wrench — air-socket wrench	0:10
X1	46-01	Hand-saw	0:14
X1	47-01	Hammering	0:11
X1	48-01	Printing-works — newspaper — press	0:50
X1	49-01	Workshop — general	1:32
X1	50-01	Adding machine — electric	0:11
X1	51-01	Duplicator — Ricoh M10	0:24
X1	52-01	Teleprinters	0:45
X1	53-01	Telephone — Bell 500 — 2 rings	0:20
X1	54-01	Telephone — Siemens — modern — 4 rings	0:17
X1	55-01	Computer printer — 400 t/s — matrixprinter	0:50
X1	56-01	Computer terminal — Apple IIE	0:46
X1	57-01	Typewriter — manual — Olympia	0:34

DIGIFFECTS   THE FULL SPECTRUM OF SOUND

Part of a compact disc sound effects library (*Courtesy of Music House International Limited*)

be recorded on one side of a disc and if the tracks are well spaced, it is easy to find a cue. Disc reproducers are capable of starting instantly from a remote switch, perhaps from an audio post-production synchronizer. However, the vinyl disc suffers from wear after continuous use and is, as such, becoming less popular. They have found particular use in current affairs and news programming where soundtracks are not laid prior to mixing, but music and effects are spun in as the mix progresses on-the-fly.

The quality of vinyl sound effects can be high, since most are pressed in small numbers where quality control can be maintained.

Compact discs

Compact discs are digitally recorded, and can provide superb sound quality. They can be started remotely and locking to time code is possible. Access is almost as good as with the vinyl disc, although rather than physically placing the pick-up arm on the disc, the CD disc is programmed to the point required.

Access to the CD disc is not instantaneous; initially, it is necessary for the reproducing laser arm to move to the track position on the disc. However, once the track point has been found, cueing is almost instantaneous. Professional machines provide shuttle facilities to find cues although the quality of the sound, in shuttle, may be somewhat limited. Any machine must be capable of accessing as many tracks as there are on disc; this usually means up to a hundred. The discs can hold up to 60 mins of material and take up only a small amount of physical space. Many manufacturers provide effects on CD discs.

Analogue tape

The quarter-inch tape has long been the traditional method of holding master sound effects recordings for libraries. Access is good, the tape can be easily spliced and one reel can hold a large amount of material. It can be easily edited to a fraction of a second, and it can also be cued with an almost instant start.

If the tape is striped with time code, access is made easier, it is merely necessary to dial in the time code relating to the sound effect for an automatic location. Although access is not instant, tape is a versatile medium and easy to lock into other systems if it is time coded.

Digital audio samplers

Digital samplers were originally designed for musicians, to allow musical sounds or notes to be sampled, electronically synthesized, looped and then played through a keyboard with pitch changes. These devices record sound on floppy discs and then convert it to RAM within the machine for playing and manipulation. The looping and pitch changing facilities of these devices have proved powerful tools in audio post-production. It is, for example, possible to store the sounds of various footsteps in a machine, and by operating a keyboard, make each key-press reproduce a footstep – its pitch being determined by its position on the keyboard. The pressure of the fingers on the keyboard affects the volume of the sound. More sophisticated keyboards and samplers allow various sound effects to be grouped onto one key. The use of these devices can considerably speed up the track laying of spot effects. Not only can footsteps be laid, but also doors opening and closing, balls hitting bats, clothes rustles, wheel skids, and similar effects that require a series of spot effects to be laid exactly in sync. By moving up and down the keyboard, the sound of an effect can be changed significantly; a small car can become a truck, small bells can become large bells etc.

Audio cartridges

The standard NAB (National Association of Broadcasters USA) audio loop cartridge can be supplied in lengths from a few seconds to many minutes. They can be recorded locally in the studio and access is good since each cartridge holds its own specific effect. However, a large library will, because of the size of the cartridges, take up a considerable amount of space. Cartridges are time consuming to make and need to be carefully monitored if the join on the loop is to be unnoticeable.

Cartridges not only run continuously, but can also be cued using tones; three cues are usually available, start, stop, and fast-rewind. They are usually capable of starting in less than 0.1 of a second and stopping in less than 0.035 of a second.

Unfortunately a cartridge machine can only run forwards, so it is impossible to find the start point of the recorded sound and then add a cue afterwards. The cue must be recorded and the sound effect started, in one action. This means the accuracy of the start of a cartridge not only depends on the machine, but also on how closely the cue tone is recorded to the start of the effect.

Synchronizer control

All these sound effect formats should be available in the audio post-production suite, and can be controlled by an audio post-production synchronizer. They may not run synchronously but can be remotely started, and cued to stop or start, at specific points called events. Time code provides an accurate trigger for these cues. The event is captured from a stationary picture or on-fly, with the videotape recorder running. Each time the captured time code figure is replayed a relay starts the appropriate audio machine. Cues like these can be trimmed for greater accuracy.

Synchronizing time coded tapes of sound effects

Much of the material used in the audio post-production suite will be recorded on time coded tapes using standard audio recorders. (These may be centre track quarter-inch machines or track half-inch machines with time code.) These machines provide a convenient way of synchronizing sounds to picture for transfer to the multitrack tape recorder. As with multitrack tape recorders these machines record time code longitudinally, which is inaccurate at slow speed or at stop. It is, therefore, impossible to find a sound on the audio machine and stop it at the appropriate point, find the relevant picture point and stop the videotape recorder, and then lock the two machines together. The machines will not run in synchronization – the audio machine being inaccurately synchronized. Other methods are therefore used:

1. The picture cue is found in still frame. The sound frame is found by rocking the tape across the heads and an approximate time code figure emerges. The tapes are then locked and run. Finally the audio tape is visually trimmed, frame by frame, against the picture until the two match.
2. The sound is cued up. The picture is run. When the picture/sound cue is reached, the soundtrack is started and the two are locked in synchronization. The synchronization is then examined and the sound is again trimmed to fit. The reaction time of the brain, from responding to the picture cue to starting the soundtrack, can be determined and automatically compensated for in the system.
3. The picture is run and on seeing the cue the video machine is stopped. The sound is run and on hearing the cue the sound is stopped. Both are then put together in synchronization. Since the brain's reaction time to both the vision and sound is the same, when both are put into synchronization they should run in near sync. The sound can again be adjusted by trimming.

Laying soundtracks

The various soundtracks are now built up on the multitrack machine. Each sound is recorded at full modulation to reduce background noise to a minimum, but, perhaps with the required 'fades in' and 'fades out'. The sounds are recorded using the synchronization and events facilities provided by the audio post-production controller. The scene to be track laid, is of a busy street with cars going by and a street vendor. It was shot mute. Like all videotape programmes the material starts with a clock counting down to the first frame of picture.

Events triggering

Firstly an appropriate background atmosphere sound is chosen from, for example, a library of NAB cartridges in the studio.

Next the start and end points of the shot are found, by moving the video player slowly to find the exact time code readings. These are loaded into the synchronizer through the keyboard as events, automatically triggering 'record in' and 'record out' points. (The events could be captured on-the-fly with the video machine running.)

The videotape and the multitrack tape recorder are then rewound. The atmosphere cartridge is started manually and track one on the multitrack is selected for the recording. The video system is started, and the synchronizer automatically puts the multitrack into 'record' at the start of the shot, and out of the end. The sound is therefore, recorded through the shot. Alternatively, the controller could programme the NAB cartridge to start and stop on the desired cue, the multitrack tape being in continuous 'record'.

Laying from tape

To lay the track of the car passing in the scene a similar technique would be used, but this time the effect is held on a location quarter-inch time coded tape. The time code reading relating to the loudest point of the car passing is captured, and the appropriate picture point is also found. These two points are then fed into the controller and synchronized up.

The synchronization of the quarter-inch tape is checked in preview mode. Should the effect be in the wrong position, the time coded audio tape is moved into 'synchronization' with the picture, by trimming. The transfer then takes place of the quarter-inch tape to the second track of the multitrack tape recorder.

Cueing by hand

The effect of a street vendor is also needed for the scene, but the position of this is not critical. Track 3 is switched to 'record' at the beginning of the scene, and at the appropriate point the street vendor effect is triggered by hand from a source, such as a CD sound effects disc. If necessary, the other two effects already recorded can be heard through the mixing desk.

Use of original location tapes

An edited video master may not include all the sounds that were available from the location tapes. Often there is insufficient track space to be able to lay all the sounds originally intended for a particular scene. These sounds need to be added in audio post-production, and synchronized to the edited picture master.

First the original location tapes (video or audio only tapes) need to be transferred, with their appropriate time codes, to a format suitable for the audio post-production suite. These tapes then need to be tied into the final picture. This is not as simple as it may at first seem, since the master original tapes and the edited master videotape no longer have the same time code. The master-editing tape will have been arbitrarily pre-striped, to allow the edited master to be built-up in the insert editing mode. Additional information is therefore necessary to tie up the two unrelated codes, but related picture and sound. Sophisticated computer controllers will give the actual offset time code figure needed to synchronize the two sounds. In less sophisticated systems it is necessary to synchronize the two together manually, by eye and ear.

Sometimes only a part of a soundtrack may exist on a video master. This will then need to be replaced and added in its entirety. For example, the sound of a car may only be laid for the length of the picture (when it is seen). However, the actual sound of the car is required to be heard coming into the picture and going away again; therefore the 'heads and tails' need to be added to complete the effect. In order to synchronize this accurately it is not necessary to have relevant time codes, only the relevant sound with synchronous code. The two soundtracks, the original and the edited version, can be synchronized by ear. A rough guess is first made of synchronization and the two are locked together. Next, both tracks are heard at once, and the original is then trimmed against the edited master. The two sounds will then merge as one, first with a slight echo, and then a phasing effect is heard – which merges into one sound and synchronization. The matching or phasing is made easier if one track is sent to one speaker, of a stereo system for example, and the other to the other speaker.

In this way tracks can be cued and laid onto the multitrack machine. The sounds are usually grouped for ease of mixing – one track containing atmosphere tracks, another track containing spot effects and another, dialogue. Once the tracks have been laid, it is difficult to move them relative to each other (they have to be re-recorded onto another machine and then re-copied back to the multitrack), so the tracks should be well planned at the start.

Splitting tracks

If sounds have been placed on inappropriate tracks their positions can be changed. This often happens with video edited masters that have been recorded with tracks butted together because of the limited track space available on the VTR machine.

The split point is found and loaded into the 'record' memory. The soundtrack is then transferred to the second track entering into 'record' at the split point. 'Record' is programmed to defeat at the end of the split. The system is then run again. This time the original butted track is programmed to 'record' but no audio is sent to the track so the original track is erased, and subsequently only exists on the second track. For the system to work well, it is necessary to get exact 'in' and 'out' record points on the tracks. Otherwise, a small portion of a frame may still exist on the original track which may be audible and distracting. The time code of these picture cuts may be available on the edit decision list (EDL), produced during the video edit.

Often, dialogue recorded on the edited video master needs to be split into two or more tracks. It may well be presented merely as one butted track with a background sound level that is different at each change of shot. In a series of interviews taken at a busy street corner, for example, none of the shots will have the same level of background traffic noise. As a result, the incoming track, at the end of an edit, is likely to 'step' in level to the next edit. This discontinuity in sound may be disturbing to the viewer. To overcome this a further soundtrack is added, which is a wild track of the background sound recorded at the location during the shooting. To help the mixing process further, the dialogue track is not left butted together but is split apart and laid alternately on to a separate track so that the sound mixer can adjust the levels of the tracks, by fading down the first track and slowly fading in the second alternating track; creating an imperceptible join. To assist the mixer even further, the heads and tails, on both these tracks, can be retrieved from the camera originals forming split sound edits, allowing a smooth mix between the two tracks to take place. This is somewhat of an ideal, for in practice interviews never seem to cut where pauses allow heads and tails to be added. However, this technique can be used in drama where lines of dialogue often begin and end in silence.

Cue sheets

As the track building takes place, cue charts or cue sheets are produced. These will specify the points at which each sound starts and finishes, together with information as to whether audio is faded in or out, mixed with another track or simply left out or cut. It may give stereo positioning information as well. The control synchronizer itself may provide a cue sheet in the form of a video display screen, the information being fed in via a keyboard and cursor. The soundtracks are now ready to be mixed.

Advantages/disadvantages of multitrack techniques

The advantages of track laying using multitrack technique are:

1. Sound levels can be controlled and set in the editing suite. This can simplify mixing.
2. Audio can be listened to in high fidelity stereo while track laying.
3. It is possible to listen to all the tracks while editing sound.
4. Audio quality is good and slightly superior to that of film (but worse than digital sound).
5. It·is possible to alter sounds electrically to make them more suitable for mixing during the track laying process (through equalization, compression etc.).
6. With computer mixing equipment it is possible to start the dubbing process while track laying.
7. It is not necessary to transfer the sound to one standard format before starting editing (as it is film).

The disadvantages of track laying using multitrack techniques are:

1. It is not possible to run a standard, analogue, audio tape recorder at slow speed and to still-frame in lock with the videotape recorder.
2. Once audio post-production has started it is very difficult to change the pictures.
3. It is necessary to off-lay the audio from the video recorder before starting.
4. Equipment is much more expensive than film editing equipment but not as expensive as that of a digital workstation.
5. The tracks arrive in the mixing area in a very basic form, since video editing time is very expensive.

6. Separate operators edit picture and lay tracks, reducing continuity of production.
7. It is time consuming to change sounds from one track to another for ease of mixing.
8. There can be problems with the build up of electronic noise.
9. Synchronizing systems only operate satisfactorily if used logically within their own operating timespan. Often, the operator is held back by the speed of the equipment, not the speed he can press the buttons.

A selection of sound effects and music libraries

A selection of sound effects and music libraries are detailed in the table below.

Table 10.1 A selection of sound effects and music libraries

Library	Country of origin	Type	Size
Bainbridge	USA	Effects	Small
BBC	GB	Effects	Medium
Bruton	GB	Music	Large
Conroy	GB	Music	Large
Chappell	GB	Music	Large
De Wolfe (Est. 1940)	GB	Music & effects	Large
Digiffects	Sweden	Effects	Large
KPM	GB	Music	Large
Network Production Music	USA	Music & effects	Medium
Soper Sound Library	USA	Music & effects	Medium
Sound Ideas	Canada	Effects	Large
Valentino (Est. 1932)	USA	Music & effects	Large
Royale	USA	Music	Small

11

Film editing

Film editing equipment is inexpensive but highly versatile. It has developed from a tradition of over fifty years of production. The industry demonstrates that high technology equipment is not always necessary to produce quality work. In fact, at times, film editing techniques can make audio multitrack operations look absurdly complicated.

Film editing is unlike video editing, primarily because during the editing stage the picture and sound are held as separate rolls of stock rather than as one combined picture and sound tape.

Film picture editing

The main item to be found in a film editing room is the editing machine. This device allows the picture to be viewed at variable speeds from still frame up to a fast speed of six times normal and more. In addition one, two or three sprocketed magnetic soundtracks can be interlocked with the picture and driven synchronously.

After a film has been shot on location, a copy or print of the camera negative is made and the location sound is transferred to sprocketed magnetic film. In the editing room the sound is synchronized with the picture. The clapperboard provides sound and picture information for matching the start of the shot. The picture is held in the editing machine's gate, at the point where the clapper is seen to hit the board, and the sound is held at the point where the clap is heard.

These too are then synchronized and run together. After the first take of the sound and picture have been synchronized, the editor runs the picture to the next clapperboard and joins the second piece of magnetic film to the first. This track is adjusted so that the second soundtrack runs in synchronization with the picture.

When the whole syncing-up process is completed, the picture and sound may be run through a numbering machine which will print, onto every foot of the picture and its appropriate soundtrack, a unique alpha-numeric code that will confirm synchronization between the image and the soundtrack.

The picture is now ready for editing, and the unwanted picture and soundtrack are cut out. Some of the sound may be stored away and later cut back into the soundtrack. The picture is now ready for spotting.

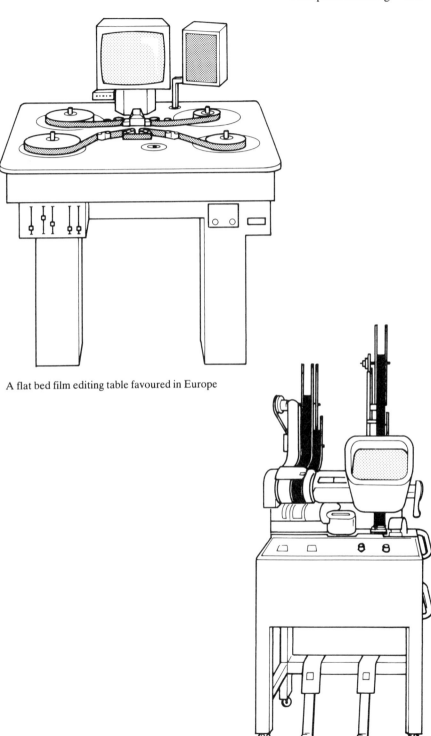

A flat bed film editing table favoured in Europe

An upright film editing machine favoured in the USA

Film track laying

The edited picture and its appropriate soundtracks are now placed in a synchronizer for sound editing. This consists of a picture viewer, connected to a series of large sprockets. These sprockets are locked on a common drive shaft which can be moved by a hand crank; a footage counter is also provided. Each of the sound sprockets, normally three, is fitted with a replay sound head connected to a small mixer. The various soundtracks are built up on this device.

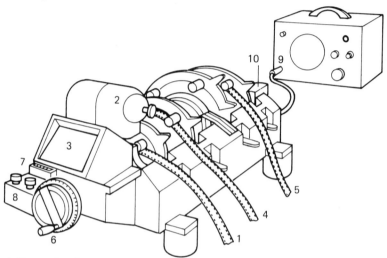

A film synchronizer

Numbered leaders are placed on each of the soundtrack wheels of the synchronizer, the soundtrack leaders being in synchronization with each other and the picture leader. The synchronizer is then wound down to the first frame of picture. At the first frame of picture, there is perhaps a scene in a city, with the sound of traffic, the effect fo a distant street vendor and a car door opening. This scene was shot mute. The appropriate rolls of magnetic film, ordered from the sound effects library, are now laid against the picture.

Since a film cutting room does not normally include any recording equipment, soundtracks that are needed for editing have to be ordered from film sound recording studios. The soundtracks are usually recorded to peak level irrespective of the volume at which they will be finally played. This keeps background noise to a minimum.

Sound editing starts at the first frame of picture on track 1. Magnetic film is spliced physically to the leader, the synchronizer winding from left to right. At this point, other tracks on the synchronizer will run off, since there is no sprocketed material after the numbered countdown head or leader. The effect for track 2 is not required for another 30 seconds, and the effect for track 3 for another 45 seconds, so additional sprocketed stock called 'leader', or 'spacer', with no oxide or emulsion on it is spliced into these tracks on the left-hand side of the synchronizer. As the synchronizer

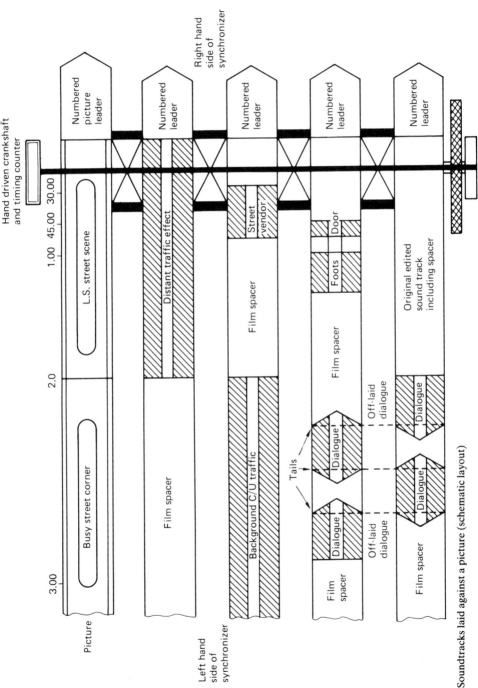

Soundtracks laid against a picture (schematic layout)

crank is turned, the soundtracks on the right-hand side remain in synchronization, together with the picture. Next, the shot of the distant street vendor is found (it is not synchronous) and the appropriate sound is cut in at approximately the right time. This is then examined to check synchronization; by listening and watching it is decided that the soundtrack is about ten frames too early. Therefore ten frames of spacer are cut into this soundtrack at the left-hand side of the synchronizer, between it and the sound effect. This means that the street vendor will be heard ten frames later. Similarly, frames could be removed at this point so that sounds are heard earlier; atmos tracks and effects are now being run together, one 'atmos' on track 1, with a separate effect on track 2.

At this point in the film we cut to a car door slamming nearby, and a character walking down the street. This was also shot mute. Our original atmosphere track is suitable for this scene since it tells the viewer that this scene is at the same location, but now we also need spot effects of a car door slamming and also footsteps.

To lay spot effects in perfect synchronization, the picture must first be carefully marked up. The exact point where the spot effect occurs is found on the picture and a mark is drawn, with a chinagraph pencil, where the car door is opened. The appropriate pieces of sound are now placed in the synchronizer and the exact points where these effects are heard on the sound stock are marked with the chinagraph. A written identification is sometimes placed on the film. The magnetic track is now placed in the synchronizer, with the chinagraph mark on the picture and the chinagraph mark on the soundtrack matched. The track is now cut into the sprocketed spacer or leader, to keep it in synchronization with the picture.

At this point the dialogue starts and is off-laid as necessary, in a similar way to soundtrack laying in video.

If the track laying is complex, the various tracks will each be categorized, as in any track laying operation, for a specific type of sound. A logical layout of the tracks will help in making any final mix-down smooth and speedy.

Loops

Sometimes there may be insufficient time to prepare a specific atmosphere track, in which case a loop of the effect may be taken to the mixing theatre where, if necessary, it can be run in synchronization with the picture.

Cue sheets

The final operation, prior to mixing the film, is to make up a cue sheet to assist the mixer during the mixing session. The cue sheet is usually prepared in the synchronizer. Before starting to prepare a cue sheet or chart, the counter on the synchronizer is zeroed to the first frame of picture after the head leader. The synchronizer then counts up frames and feet in 35 mm film, 16 mm film or time; as the crank is turned.

	Picture	Track one	Track two	Track three	Track four
0000.00 15 secs	Street scene	Distant traffic effect			
30 secs					
45 secs			Street vendor	Door	
1 min				Foots	
2 mins	Busy street corner and dialogue		Background traffic	Dialogue Dialogue	Dialogue Dialogue
3 mins					

Film cue sheet

The advantages/disadvantages of track laying using sprocketed magnetic film

The advantages of track laying using sprocketed magnetic film are:

1. It is possible to still the picture in the gate with the soundtrack held in exact synchronization.
2. The film generates no audio noise when the soundtrack is silent, since leader is cut between the recordings, not magnetic film.
3. It is possible to make up an unlimited number of tracks (perhaps even up to one hundred with a feature film), and pre-mix any selection of them.
4. Loops can be made instantly in the cutting-room, and can be run in synchronization with the picture.

5. It is possible to physically mark the picture with cues, using chinagraph pencils, and to then change them.
6. The equipment required for soundtrack cutting is inexpensive and easy to understand.
7. It is highly flexible.

The disadvantages of track laying using sprocketed film are:

1. There is no check of technical quality while laying the tracks.
2. It is impossible to change the quality or level of the sound at the tracklaying stage.
3. It is sometimes difficult to judge the suitability of sounds both stereo and mono because of the limited quality of the cutting equipment.
4. Since there are no recording facilities in the cutting-rooms, it can be time consuming to change sounds since these have to be ordered from elsewhere.
5. Sounds recorded in the field cannot be played back instantly in the cutting-room without first being transferred, to sprocketed film.
6. Although soundtracks should not lose sync, when this does happen, there is no specific time code reference to match picture and soundtrack (unless the film and soundtrack have already been rubber or frame numbered).
7. When laying sound, only two or three of the tracks laid can be heard at the one time.

It is argued that the video/multitrack tracklaying process is expensive because of the high costs of equipment, whereas the magnetic film process is relatively inexpensive since cheap simple equipment is used. It is possible to lay soundtracks with sprocketed magnetic film against video pictures.

Hybrid film and video track laying systems

To lay sprocketed film soundtracks against a video picture, the film equipment is fitted with a generator which delivers synchronizing pulses. These pulses are fed into a micro-processor which controls the video machine (a U-matic) which is driven as a slave. If vertical interval time code is used on the video master, the system will run successfully at slow speeds and hold synchronization in still frame. The system can be fitted to a film synchronizer or to a standard film editing table.

Track laying is carried out in the normal film manner. First the original audio from the master edited videotape is transferred synchronously to sprocketed film. At the same time the master videotape is dubbed onto a low cost video format with vertical internal time code. The sprocketed film can be cut as required and, if necessary, the original sound video masters can, also, be transferred to sprocketed film for sound editing.

The process follows the standard sprocketed magnetic film editing procedures. After the soundtrack has been mixed and completed, it is matched to the edited video master.

Tele-recording

An alternative to connecting a videotape recorder to a sprocketed magnetic editing machine is to transfer the videotape to film. This film (or tele-recording), can then be used on a normal film editing machine. The sprocketed soundtrack, transferred from the video master, is synchronized against it; when the final mix is complete the soundtrack is transferred back to the videotape.

12

Work stations

Work stations record sound digitally on computer discs. They try to unify all the stages of film and video sound post-production. They are capable of storing, recording, editing, mixing and processing sound as well as reproducing it for immediate play-back, but the facilities offered vary enormously from manufacturer to manufacturer. They take advantage of both film and multitrack techniques and are purely an audio post-production device not a picture editing tool. They will interface with any film or video formats, but are usually locked to the U-matic video format. Their speed of operation is dependent on the lock-up speed of the picture machine.

The facilities work stations offer differ considerably, depending on their concept and their price. The following description relates to most, but not all, on the market:

Like any audio post-production system, with work stations a degree of preparation is necessary before starting audio mixing: the system must be loaded up with sound from the video or film edited master (complete with any relevant time code). If the production is shot separate-sound, the original master recordings complete with their time code must also be loaded into the machines and, in addition, an edit decision list is required to synchronize these tapes back to the master edited videotape. The work station may include its own sound effects library or it may alternatively be necessary to order effects specially and load the machine with them later. As the sound effects are entered they are labelled, producing a specific library for the production. The access to this is almost instant.

Information for the work station is shown on a video display unit with control from such devices as a keyboard, a touch-sensitive screen, or a cursor. The various visual displays are usually available, individually or together.

Cue sheet

The electronic cue sheet controls the system. The editor enters into the display the library number of the sounds to be played and the point it is to be played at. Some cue sheets display pictorial representations of the soundtrack similar to the modulations of an optical film soundtrack.

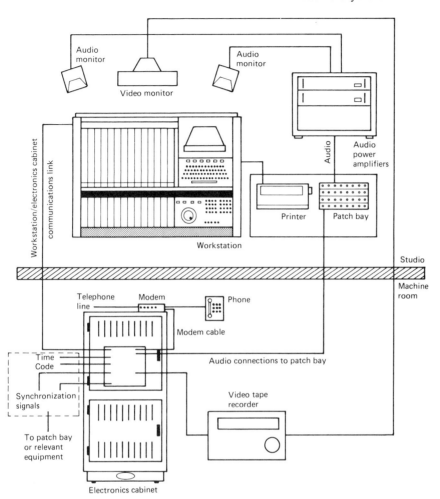

A workstation with its control electronics

Meter screen

The meter screen helps check sound processing levels such as volume, reverberation or panning. As the sounds are played the screen displays in real time, the automation level set for each channel, the curves for frequency equalization, dynamics etc.

The library screen

The library screen displays text and graphic information on the sounds loaded into the system. They are labelled, numbered, and located by time code information, and are transferred to the cue sheet for manipulating.

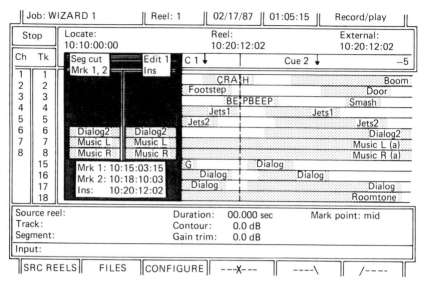

A cue display screen (*Courtesy of F W O Bauch Limited and Lexicon Opus*)

Job: WIZARD 1	Reel: 1		02-17-87	12:10:20	Hard disk files
Job/reel/trk	Segments	Duration	Date/time		Comments
WIZARD 1			1/05/87, 11:25		
Reel 1		00:10:45:00	2/12/87, 8:25		
Track 1		00:10:45:00	2/12/87, 8:25		
	Bang	00:00:01:20	2/12/87, 8:35		
	Crash	00:00:03:25	2/12/87, 8:37		
	Boom	00:00:04:27	2/12/87, 8:38		
	Footstep	00:00:02:05	2/12/87, 8:40		
	Door	00:00:01:17	2/12/87, 8:41		
	Beepbeep	00:00:01:02	2/12/87, 8:43		
	Smash	00:00:02:07	2/12/87, 8:45		
	Jets 1	00:00:03:06	2/12/87, 8:48		

Total disk time: 120 track minutes. Time used: 3 reels, 50 minutes used.
Time available: 70 track minutes

Full text:

Input:

| REC/PLY | NEWJOB/REEL | CONFIGURE | SEL DRIVE | TRANSFER | LOG IN |

A library screen (*Courtesy of F W O Bauch Limited and Lexicon Opus*)

Technical screens

Other screens are often available giving technical information such as the signal routing and configuration, the synchronization interfaces with time code, the digital sampling rate diagnostic programmes for maintenance and so on.

Using the work station

Initially the video display unit is selected to show the cue sheet. This consists of a picture track for showing the picture cuts, with facilities for notes to be written in, together with the audio track, that can be labelled appropriately.

The motion controls are of the standard type, fast forward, fast rewind and play and record. When 'play' is selected, the cue sheet moves across a time line point which represents the tape head. This is the point at which the audio is triggered, and the time code is always displayed. When sound is edited onto the cue sheet it is highlighted as blocks or shown as modulations and each sound can be individually labelled. In the first instance the cue sheet will display the sound from the edited video master, which has been off-laid into the work station. This sound can be split and laid onto separate tracks or alternatively, matched where necessary to the original separate sound that has been transferred to the work station's library.

When it is required to split an edited track from the video master into separate tracks, the first operation is to move the picture to the cut point, the audio following precisely in lock. Next the system is told, perhaps via a keyboard or cursor to move the sound on track 1, at the assigned cut point, to track 2 and hold it. In this way a butted dialogue track can be off-laid onto the various tracks of the system. The cueing is accurate to better than one frame, and any point can be accurately found using the controls. Using similar techniques it is possible to fit wild recordings of dialogue into close synchronization.

If it is necessary to go back to the original sound masters which are held within the library, these can be selected from the library page. The sound effect is identified by its time code or label and then triggered so that it can be heard. Once the sound has been found the video display unit is returned to its cue sheet page; the sound is assigned to a track where it is shown as a long moving block. This sound can then be moved into precise synchronization with the picture and locked in and recorded at the correct point. Should time code information be available to synchronize the sound directly with its picture, this too can be achieved at the touch of a button. Should it be necessary to cut the sound at the end of the picture cut, this point can be found on the picture, and the system can erase the sound from the desired point. Obviously sounds from the library can be moved to any point required. Although sounds can be recorded and moved around the cue sheet, none of the sounds from the library are erased so they can be used as many times as is required. Work stations can also make up loops of sound with perfect joins. Some even offer piano-type keyboards to retrieve and lay spot sound effects such as footsteps, door slams etc.

The advantages of work stations are:

1. Sound remains in the digital domain and is therefore of the highest quality.
2. Access is instant (although this will depend on how full the system is).
3. Auto conforming with the original separate sound is possible within the system provided the edited video master holds the original time codes.

4. The system can shuttle in synchronization at slow speeds and park in synchronization, although it may be restricted by the stationary accuracy of the interlocked video machine.
4. Improvements and updates are easy to incorporate in the system by changing software.
5. It is possible to diagnose faults via a telephone line through a 'modem' to increase maintenance efficiency. (The system is directly interfaced to the telephone line).

The disadvantages of work stations are:

1. The system is expensive.
2. The capacity can be limited and depends on price.
3. Work has to be loaded into the system.
4. It may not be possible to remove the stored data discs physically from the system, making it necessary to copy 'archive' material out of the work station.
5. It requires new operating skills; systems are not operationally compatible.
6. It is highly complex technology.

13

Stereo

Stereo sound is found in most domestic environments, CD discs, albums and the radio are almost always stereo, and even archive material tends to be simulated stereo. Television, however, may or may not be originated in stereo.

Stereophonic sound conveys information about the location of sound sources, but this ability to provide directional information is only one of the advantages of stereophony. Stereo recordings have an improvement in realism and clarity over mono recordings. They have a clearer distinction between the direct and reflected sounds which produces a spacious 3-dimensional image with a better ambient field. Pictures can be powerfully reinforced by the use of stereo sound with better directional cues for off stage action, and with sound effects which have increased depth and definition.

Even television with its small sound field benefits from stereo sound. The positioning of sounds may not be practical but the re-creation of an acoustic can, it is argued, be used advantageously. In a multi-camera production it might be impractical to position the microphone correctly for each shot in a rapidly cutting sequence. However, it is claimed that a general stereo acoustic can give a satisfactory result, particularly in sports and current affairs programmes.

Recording stereo sound requires more equipment and more tracks. Post-production time is increased and there are small increases in recording time on location or on the set. Thus stereo productions are more expensive to produce than those made in mono, both in terms of time and in equipment needed.

Stereo dialogue

AB coincident pair technique

It is said that the best stereo sound is produced using a pair of microphone capsules with cardioid response separated by about 6 inches at an angle of 110 degrees. The sound arrives at capsule A at a different time to capsule B. There is a phase shift difference between the sound arriving at the two microphones, depending on frequency (which will also depend on

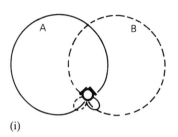 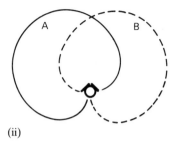

(i)   (ii)

Polar diagrams for polar microphones used as a stereo pair; (i) A crossed pair of cottage loaf polar diagram micrphones; (ii) A crossed pair of cardioid polar diagram microphones

direction) and the acoustics of the environment. It is this which produces the stereo effect.

This AB co-incident pair technique is not suitable for television and film production dialogue recording – it is too critical to set up and takes time to arrange successfully. Using this type of microphone technique produces dramatic changes in the stereo image when a microphone is racked in and out on a boom across a set; the effect is inconsistent with the picture and may not be compatible in mono.

Spaced microphone technique

The spaced microphones technique is sometimes used to record stereo for television and film. The microphones cover the sound field at a distance from each other and this can produce excellent effects recording, particularly of moving objects. This technique is advisable for motion picture stereo matrix systems, where two spaced microphones help to reduce the tendency of phase incompatibility in mono.

It can be used for dialogue recording, but needs even more careful setting up than the A/B co-incident format.

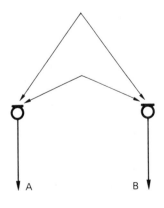

A A   B   A spaced pair of stereo microphones

M & S microphone technique

It is possible to replace the two cardioid microphones in the co-incident pair with two figure of eight microphones and again produce effective stereo; but this again is unsatisfactory from an operational point of view.

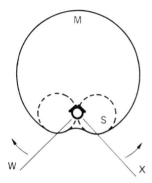

The response of a figure of eight and a cardioid microphone used in the mid plus side format. A special matrix is needed to decode the signal to a left and right format

However, by using a figure of eight microphone and a cardioid microphone and then reversing the phase of one of the microphones and moving it 45 degrees to the other, a very effective 'cardioid' stereo pickup is available. One microphone will pick up the sound 'in the middle' and the other pick up sound 'sideways'. The output from this stereo combination is called M and S respectively – Mid and Side.

Tradition has it that the positive north lobe or pick-up pattern, of the M, is kept in phase with the positive S lobe of the side. The angle between these lobes can be varied by altering the proportion of the side signal to 'centre', thus offering control over the width of the image. A matrix is required to decode the recording into a standard left plus right system.

The system has several advantages:

1. Since the mono signal is produced from a single microphone, the problems of mono incompatibility are fewer.
2. The width of the stereo image can be varied to match the picture by the ratio of the M to S signal.
3. The control of image width can help match sound, shot to shot.
4. The mono signal can be monitored and recorded in the normal manner with the side signal recorded on track 2, which can be ignored except for the occasional checking.
5. Phase errors in the system produce only a change in width which is less disturbing than 'image-wobble' which other systems possess. In the case of complete phase reversal, one channel only will result, the image being changed from left to right. If there are phase and level problems in a M & S recording, the result is a loss of separation. (On portable tape recorders the small size of the meters does not allow easy, accurate line-up, and extreme care must be taken when setting up recording levels for M and S recording.)

M & S is an excellent microphone technique to use in recording dialogue if little or no post-production is to take place. It produces consistent results and can always be reverted to mono if the stereo produced is unacceptable. Unfortunately, the signals have to be de-coded into normal left and right stereo. This means that a matrix has to be used for monitoring on location and in the audio post-production suite.

There are further problems if a microphone boom is used. In mono it is normal practice to favour the artiste speaking by panning the microphone head. If this is attempted with a stereo microphone the stereo sound field will be heard to move, although the picture will remain static, thus a compromise position has to be found. Therefore, in mono reproduction some artistes are 'off mic' and subject to increased background noise – this is a general problem with stereo. Unfortunately, this noise also includes more concentrated sounds as well as ambient stereo sounds, such as camera noise, tracking noise, traffic, etc. In addition, all stereo recordings can suffer from some phase problems which mono will not. Some would argue therefore, that where audio post-production is involved, properly recorded mono dialogue is of more value than stereo dialogue, provided that good stereo sound effects and music are available.

In the motion picture industry dialogue is always recorded in mono and occasionally it is moved from the centre of screen to the sides for dramatic effect. In fact the matrix used to record stereo in motion picture work is in some respects phase dependent. Thus, the dialogue recorded in stereo may be unsatisfactorily reproduced, (phase similarities tend to narrow the stereo image). The motion picture industry tends to create stereo by careful track laying and mixing, rather than by original stereo dialogue and effects recording. Music is always recorded in stereo, possibly with additional channels that can be added to create a special effect during the mix. The spots effects are often in mono as are other single source sounds, which are moved to position across the sound field by panning, but atmospheres and other multi source sound effects may well be recorded in stereo.

For simple video stereophonic productions the television industry records much of its original sound in stereo.

Track laying and stereo

Stereo soundtracks are track laid and mixed in a similar way to mono ones, but there is the additional advantage of being able to position the sound in the sound field during the recording and mixing process. To ease re-recording problems, it is important that the same stereo recording format is used wherever possible, so that, for example, an M & S system is not butt joined, or close to, an incompatible A/B stereo recording. It is important also, to check that moving sounds originally track laid in stereo, match their moving pictures. A train, for example, should be laid moving left to right – if the train is shown in the picture moving left to right (although its direction can be changed in the mix).

Physical joins on stereo material, whether it be film or tape, must be particularly carefully made, otherwise the stereo image may wobble as the join passes the heads. Stereo recordings should, wherever possible, be made on tracks that are physically next to each other, so as to reduce the possibilities of phase errors on tracks that are some distance apart.

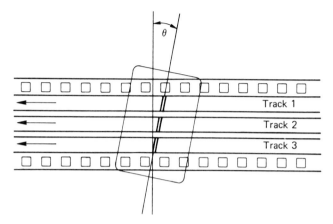

An azimuth error on a 35 mm magnetic film head magnified by using tracks one and three creating greater phase problems than by using adjacent tracks (see also page 142)

The major problem with stereo is that it increases the number of tracks needed, since each stereo sound requires two tracks. In track laying film, this is not necessarily a problem since two separate tracks are available on every gauge of sprocketed stock. However, within the multitrack tape and work station systems the number of tracks available is limited, and this reduces the facilities available.

In videotape systems, the need for two audio tracks for one stereo sound creates problems even with simple editing. No longer is it possible to use both tracks of the videotape recorder for laying different sounds. A two-track machine now only has available one soundtrack for the picture. To extend the number of soundtracks available, it is necessary.

1. To use other tracks on the videotape, as on the 1 inch C format.
2. To edit the videotape sound in mono, and using this track as a guide, with the edit decision list, to lay back the stereo sound from the stereo master.
3. To lock a separate sound machine to the videotape recorder while editing. This is perhaps the most effective method.

Stereo audio synthesizers

It is sometimes necessary to recreate stereo from mono, either in audio post-production or at a transmitter, in an attempt to maintain a 'stereo' output even when mono is being reproduced. Devices to produce this 'pseudo stereo' sound have been available for a number of years.

The earliest attempts at producing a stereo image from a mono sound source were made in the late 1940s in Germany, the system developed used a high pass filter on one channel and a low-pass filter on the other. This gave the illusion of the bass instruments of an orchestra coming from one side of the sound field and the treble instruments coming from another.

This was developed into a more sophisticated system of two interleaved comb filters; one for the left and one for the right. The combs fall at random intervals, and if they are heard together in mono, no audio coloration is noticeable. Instead of comb filters it is possible to use frequency band filters. But in this case it is difficult to construct interleaving frequency bands that do not add coloration to the sound when reproduced in mono.

Time delays are also used to produce pseudo stereo, but if the delay times are not carefully controlled mono incompatibility will result.

Stereo synthesizers are designed to process both mono dialogue and music into stereo, but they are, however, far more effective with music. Speech tends to be monotonic, with a disembodied quality, and this means the depth and width controls provided cannot be used to their fullest extent. The exception is dialogue recorded in a very reverberant acoustic, where full width and depth control increases intelligibility and appears to reduce the background reverberation.

14

Music

Music has always been a vital part of the film and television soundtrack. It is used as a creator of atmosphere, mood, or emotion, and appears in almost all types of productions, whether they be motion picture films for theatrical release or simple television productions, which merely have title music. Title music will provide the mood of a production, background music will provide the atmosphere and drama. More recently, music video promotions have used the techniques of audio post-production to produce special music mixes with synchronized sound effects.

Music is laid into soundtracks in exactly the same way as sound effects. Just as certain tracks are designated to sound effects, so certain soundtracks will be designated to music. Similarly, music can be specially recorded or can be ordered from specialist libraries.

Use of music

Whatever type of music is used, it must be placed at the right point for the right reasons. The most frequent failure in music editing is placing music in the wrong place, for the wrong purposes. It is important to recognize where the principal impact of music should be in a particular scene. Where does it come in? When does the music go out? Perhaps it can be sneaked in unobtrusively, using a sound effect to mask the entrance. Alternatively, it might be introduced on a dialogue cue in a quiet, reflective or even thunderous mood. Entrances can be understated, overstated, or just stated.

Action and sound effects are good counterpoints to music and can be highly dramatic, expressing the emotions of characters rather than merely accompanying them with the speed of the action. However, over impressive sounds can detract from the pictures. Loud music is also undesirable since, unless it is carefully composed and positioned, it will need to be held down low under other sounds. It is important to avoid excessive high-frequency content in music too, since, if this is held down in the mixing stage, the music will lose its body and characteristics.

It is essential that music does not fight with dialogue or effects. Small ensembles of strings or woodwind for example, work well behind dialogue providing they are in careful register and timbre, but a significant change in level does not usually work unless the music is punctuating the dialogue to produce an effect. Perhaps the most startling effect is sudden silence. Halting the music and playing the moment of drama in silence, can be intensely effective.

Music especially composed for a production

If music is to be especially written for a production the composer and director will first decide on the sections that are to have music written over them. The composer will be given a video copy of the edited material, in as near a fine cut version as possible, with burnt-in time code and possibly a track, giving the proposed tempo. This may be a recording of a piece of music similar in feeling to the type required.

Until the introduction of the domestic video cassette recorder, composers only had a limited time to view their films or programmes and to prepare notes for composition. Since the introduction of the domestic VCR, composers have been able to view whenever they wish and even construct tracks using computers at home, and then take the time coded videotape and computer information to the studio for the mix.

Music in audio post-production is classically divided into two distinct types, source music, and music scored for dramatic effect.

Source music comes from an actual source on the screen. This may be visual or just implied. People dancing to a 'live' band is scored with 'visual' source music, but if the band is playing on the radio, it is 'implied' source music. This music can be developed into part of the framework of a film and it may then become the score of the production. Often the theme is set up in the main title and from then on is used wherever appropriate.

Dramatic scoring is the most usual form of musical scoring. Basically, here, the music is being used in a theatrical way – the composer has complete freedom to decide upon how the music is written and how he portrays the emotions of the production.

Once the composer's ideas have been approved, and the final cut has been completed, the music recording session will be scheduled. This is usually the last operation before the final soundtrack mix; the music may or may not be recorded with the picture.

Music recording to picture

In this method, the completed final cut of the scene to be recorded is viewed by the conductor and the musicians as they perform the work. The film or the videotape is marked with cues to indicate to the conductor when the music is about to begin and end. Through headphones he, and possibly the musicians, will hear the click track, or an electronic metronome dictating the tempo or the exact required beat of the music, (tempos are expressed in frames rather than in metronome beats). Cued from time code or film footage readings, the click track runs in synchronization with the picture. It can be started at a number of clicks prior to the first frame of picture so as to give a count-in to the musicians; the click generator can be programmed to speed up or slow down at the appropriate point with the picture.

When synthesizers are a major source of music in a production, the picture time code is locked to the synthesizers' midi code. This allows a number of keyboards, electronic drum machines etc., to be accurately controlled to the picture time code. Computers of this type can also calculate tempos, real and relative timings, set accelerandos and retards to hit cues at the correct time, and do all the paperwork necessary for music recording to picture. All these systems have been developed for the home studio as well as the music recording studio.

The ease of synchronizing video recorders and multitrack audio machines has led specialist music recording studios to offer music/picture recording facilities to the audio post-production industry. These studios specialize in recording music that is to be reproduced in the home environment and this provides the ideal for television work. However, recordings made for the domestic environment may not be suitable for reproduction in a cinema.

Music for motion pictures

Stereo mixes for the cinema need to be monitored on at least the three main channels, left, centre, and right. This means there is incompatibility with stereo music mixes that have been specifically recorded for two channel systems – such as for the home. These tend to sound too narrow when played in a theatrical environment, because the coding matrix used in the cinema tends to pull the sides of a stereo image to the centre. This problem can be eliminated by monitoring through a matrix unit, allowing multiple speakers to be used during the recording session (simulating a matrix recording). Ideally, these multitrack tapes should be mixed together in a film mixing stage where the acoustic characteristics are correct for reproducing in a cinema, and the monitoring level is set to the recommended standard.

Often it is impossible to record music to picture. Perhaps the recordings have to be completed before the final edit, or perhaps there is insufficient finance for an expensive picture recording session. In this situation the music is recorded 'wild', and eventually a certain amount of music editing will be necessary to fit the music to the pictures. If the music is to be part of a series, 'atmospheres' will be composed that can be used at the appropriate times. Obviously, title music and credit music, together with breaks, are needed, and in addition to this, chase, comedy, fight and dramatic stings for example, are recorded, all to be placed in the appropriate positions by the editor.

Sometimes music cannot be specially recorded for a production and in this case mood music libraries are often used to provide a suitable alternative. Most mood music publishers issue a detailed catalogue listing the tapes, albums and compact discs they are able to supply. The selection is enormous. Almost every type of instrument, orchestra, or national sound can be supplied, to any mood, whether it is lighthearted or dramatic,

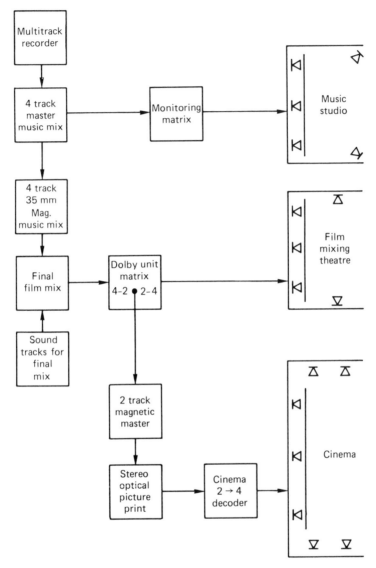

Music recording (Four track master) for the cinema using the Dolby SVA matrix system (see also page 138)

rock or funky. These 'non-commercial' libraries are being continually updated and follow fashion well.

Complicated editing and animation sequences requiring music are usually edited to already recorded compositions. This allows the picture editor the opportunity to illustrate the music and exploit the musical rhythm as he wishes. These techniques are always used in animation where musical tempo is used to structure the sequence.

DISC LIST

Number	Title	Composer	Description
DWCD 0001	MIRAGE	Andy Quin	Bright Modern innovative sounds for Action Sport and Industry featuring The Fairlight Computer Musical Instrument
DWCD 0002	RENOIR	A May/B Alberici/R Tilsley	A Selection of Melodic Pieces for Large Orchestra and Small Group featuring Piano
DWCD 0003	NIGHT CRUISIN	Paul Westwood	A Selection of Up-to-date Pieces for Small Group and Brass played by Unit 9
DWCD 0004	CONSTELLATION	Simon Park	Large Orchestral Pieces for Action, Achievement, Industry etc played by the International Television Orchestra
DWCD 0005	NEW IMAGES	David Hubbard	A Selection of Modern Synthesized Pieces suitable for Action and Industry, played by Unit 2
DWCD 0006	CUTS FOR COMMERCIALS VOL 3	K Jenkins/M Ratledge	A Selection of Music for Electronic Keyboards recorded in Commercial Lengths
DWCD 0007	SLAVE DRIVER	F McDonald/C Rae	Modern Group sounds featuring Electric Guitars, played by Blue Steel
DWCD 0008	THE NEW WORLD	Tim Souster	A Selection of Dramatic Orchestral Pieces played by The Royal Philharmonic Orchestra
DWCD 0009	INTERSTATE	S Heseley	Optimistic Modern Orchestral Themes with Commercial Lengths
DWCD 0010	TOUCH OF A BUTTON	Andy Quin	Colourful Energetic Themes played on The Fairlight Computer Musical Instrument
DWCD 0011	WITHIN RANGE	A Hobson	Modern Orchestral Themes with Commercial Lengths played by The International Television Orchestra
DWCD 0012	OVER THE MOON	A Hobson	Modern Group sounds featuring Synthesizers and Brass played by Unit 9
DWCD 0013	SPIRIT OF AMERICA	S Heseley/T Souster/G Todd	Large Orchestral Themes depicting the American Way of Life played by The Royal Philharmonic Orchestra
DWCD 0014	FACETS	A Hobson	Modern Orchestral and Synthesized Pieces for Titles, Industry and Achievement
DWCD 0015	MEET THE FUTURE	A Hobson/M Miers	Modern Large Group sounds featuring Brass and Guitars, for Sport and Action
DWCD 0016	TOPSY TURVY	J Trombey/ K Jenkins	Lighthearted Pieces for Small Group suitable for Children, Games and Fun
DWCD 0017	VIDEOTRONICS	Andy Quin	An Orchestral Approach to the Fairlight CMI – Dynamic and Prestigious music for Audio Visual and Video Production
DWCD 0018	CLASSICS ONE	Simon Park	Classical Music for Full Orchestra, Chamber Orchestra and Organ with Strings
DWCD 0019	VIDEOTRONICS TWO	Andy Quin	Dynamic, Prestigious music for Audio Visual and Video Production using Fairlight CMI
DWCD 0020	LIFE BY NIGHT	Nick Ingman	Large Orchestral Pieces featuring Acoustic Guitar suitable for Leisure and Holidays
DWCD 0021	CHALLENGE THE WORLD	S Park/D Way	Large, Modern Orchestral Pieces for Sport, Action and Achievement
DWCD 0022	SWITCHCRAFT	R Jackson/C Blackwell	Bright, Innovative Electronic Keyboard and Sampled sounds for Audio Visual and Video Production
DWCD 0023	SILICON VALLEY	A Hobson/T Bastow	A Look at the World of High Technology featuring Electronic Keyboards
DWCD 0024	CLASSICS TWO	S Park/D Way	Classical Music in a Variety of Styles for Full Orchestra and Organ with Strings
DWCD 0025	THE CUTTING EDGE	Andy Quin	Contemporary music for keyboards and sampling machines with the emphasis on rhythm and percussion
DWCD 0026	PRIME CUTS VOLUME ONE	Andy Quin	A Selection of Short Pieces for Commercials with and without Sound Effects for Small Group
DWCD 0027	SCREAM & SCREAM AGAIN	Tim Souster	Large Orchestral Dramatic and Sinister Impressions
DWCD 0028	JUST WHIMSICAL	A Hobson/C Evans-Ironside	Lighthearted Small Group Moods featuring Bassoon and Keyboards
DWCD 0029	MULTIPLE IMAGE	Chris Evans-Ironside	Interesting, Colourful Electronic Keyboard Music for Audio Visual and Video Production
DWCD 0030	EVENING CALM	J Answell/P Lewis	Pastoral Impressions for Small Group featuring Woodwind
DWCD 0031	LIFESTYLE	J Collins/M Harrison	Modern Small Group Music featuring Saxophone and Keyboards suitable for Leisure and City Life
DWCD 0032	EDDIE THE RAZOR	Eddie Jones	Small Group Music featuring Guitar and Piano in Rock, Rock 'n' Roll and Boogie Styles
DWCD 0033	DISCOVERIES	John Hyde	Modern Electronic Music featuring Trumpet and Guitars with the accent on Rhythm and Percussion

Part of a music library available in Compact Disc (*Courtesy of De Wolfe Limited*)

Musical programmes

Recordings of live performances of musical works have to be carefully mixed so that they appear to match the pictures, although it is often impossible for the sound to slavishly follow the shots. In a reverse angle, for example from the rear of the stage, the stereo image would need to be reversed to be 'realistic'. Nevertheless it is important, that what is clearly seen is clearly heard. The ambience of the sound must fit the apparent acoustics of the location. In a concert hall, for example, the sound heard from the auditorium will often appear to be too distant for close-up pictures, so a closer perspective is required. Certain specific effects may be positioned to match pictures, and this technique is often used in rock music shows.

Copyright

All creative works are held in copyright by their owners, whether they be sound effects, recordings, scripts, music, or whatever. To make use of such works, the user is liable to pay a fee. Usually the fee allows limited use of the work rather than an outright sale, although contracts for outright sale are not usual for the purchase of sound effects.

Sound effects are licensed directly by their owners but scripts may be licensed-out by agents as well as writers. Music rights are controlled by specific organizations set up, particularly, to deal with contracts and copyright. They take vigorous action in defence of their clients, who often give them complete control over copyright collection.

Copyright law is complex and varies from country to country but there are reciprocal agreements to allow copyright to be administered across national boundaries. Copyright clearance should be obtained prior to using any work. In recorded music, clearance often needs to be obtained from the composer, the owner of the recording of the music, the owner of copyright held in the performing of the music, and the owner of copyright held in the broadcasting of the piece.

The fees payable will depend on how large the audience is for the proposed production. Will it be only shown for industrial use? This would incur a small fee. Alternatively, will it be for worldwide television distribution? This would require a large fee.

Organizations concerned with music clearance include:

The Americal Society of Composers Authors and Publishers (ASCAP)
Broadcast Music Incorporated (BMI)
The Harry Fox Agency, (USA)
Mechanical Copyright Protection Society (MCPS)
Performing Rights Society (PRS)
Phonographic Performances Limited (PPL)
Society of European State Authors and Composers (SESAC)

15

Monitoring and the environment

Soundtracks are reproduced in various different acoustic environments; the home, the cinema, the conference hall. The mark of a well mixed soundtrack is one that can be heard intelligibly in all these different situations.

In the ideal world, all control rooms and listening rooms would be standardized, to allow perfect recordings to be heard. However, they are not, and since sound is very subjective, and since no two people are likely to interpret sound in the same way, it is surprising that there is any similarity between recorded sounds at all. A control room for monitoring sound must possess certain characteristics:

The control room

1. The sound balance recorded in the room should not sound any different when played back in other environments.
2. As a listener moves around the room, the sound quality should not change noticeably.
3. When listening at normal listening levels, it should be possible to hear the background noise level of the recording medium, enabling a check to be made on the build-up of noise through the system (although this is unlikely to be possible with digital recording).

In the audio post-production control room, decisions are made during the sound mix on:

1. Artistic judgements of levels, perspective of sounds, fades, dissolves and cuts.
2. Correct synchronization, making sure there is the correct time relationship between spot effects, dialogue, music etc.
3. Technical quality concerning the acceptable 'wow' and 'flutter' frequency response, phase errors and noise and distortion of the system.
4. Placement of the stereo image, making sure that the sound moves correctly in relationship to the pictures across the stereo field.
5. Stereo compatibility with mono, making sure that the viewers in mono receive an intelligible signal.

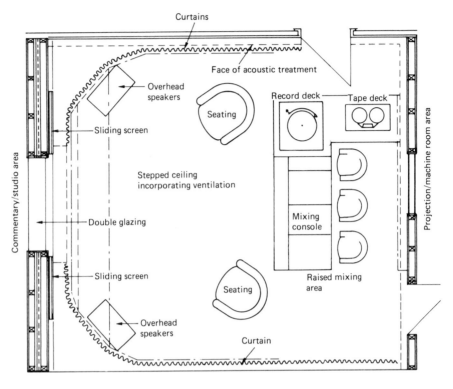

A small mono mixing theatre designed for film productions made for television

Monitoring loudspeakers

The most important instrument in the audio post-production studio is the loudspeaker; from it, everything is judged. It has been said that loudspeakers are windows through which we view sound images, and this is a fairly apt analogy. However, sounds are more difficult than pictures to interpret correctly; an experienced eye can easily check the colour-balance of a colour photograph by comparing it with the original. Sound, however, is open to a more subjective interpretation, being influenced by acoustics, reverberation, loudspeaker distance, and level. All these affect the quality of sound we perceive through the window of our loudspeaker.

Loudspeakers are notoriously difficult to quantify. Terms such as harshness, definition, lightness, crispness and the more modern term, translucence, are commonly used. But these different terms have different meanings for different people; stereo adds yet one more dimension to the problem.

For stereo monitoring, matched speakers are essential to ensure a consistent sound image across the monitoring window.

Stereo monitoring

Stereo is used in audio post-production in three specific formats:

1. The simple left right stereo format used in stereo television (two separate discrete channels).
2. The cinema left, right and centre with ambient format, used in Dolby optical stereo (SVA) (a matrix encoded system recorded on two tracks).
3. The six track stereo magnetic format of 70 mm (six discrete magnetic tracks on the picture print).

If stereo recordings are to be satisfactorily monitored, the sound image reproduced needs to have a fixed relationship to the picture. It is important, therefore, that there are sufficient sources across the sound field. In the cinema, where the width of the screen is perhaps fifteen metres, at least three speakers are required to reproduce the sound satisfactorily, but in television, where the picture image is smaller, a pair of speakers positioned either side of the screen, produces a satisfactory image.

It is generally recommended that in domestic two channel hi-fi stereo sound systems, the speakers are placed at angles of 60 degrees to the listener. Smaller angles make it difficult to judge the stability of the centre (or so-called phantom) image, and larger angles can remove the centre image almost completely (leaving 'a hole in the middle'). At angles of 60 degrees the listener and speakers are equally and ideally spaced from each other, the listener sitting at the corners of an equilateral triangle. This system has been adapted for television, where there is the additional requirement that the visual field and the sound must relate. Experience has shown that the width of the screen should be repeated between the edge of the screen and the loudspeaker beside it. This allows a conventional 60 degree pattern in a reasonably sized room. The room should be acoustically symmetrical from left to right, so that sound does not change as it moves from one speaker to another.

In a studio control room this set-up may not be ideal, for only one person may be able to sit in the correct listening position – a slight movement of the head leading to a significant change in the stereo image. This situation can be improved by far-field monitors with a larger sound field, allowing more people to hear the stereo image. This sound field is, however, more likely to be influenced by the acoustic characteristics of the room. If near field monitoring is used, the loudspeaker systems need an exceptionally smooth frequency response over the acoustic area.

Acoustics and reverberation

Reverberation affects the quality of reproduced sound and so it is a vital consideration in the design of any sound listening room, whether it be a studio or a cinema. Reverberation time is measured by the time taken for a sound pressure to drop by 60 db; this can vary between 0.2 and 1 second depending on the size and the treatment of a studio. This reverberation time, however, must be the same at all frequencies to produce a good

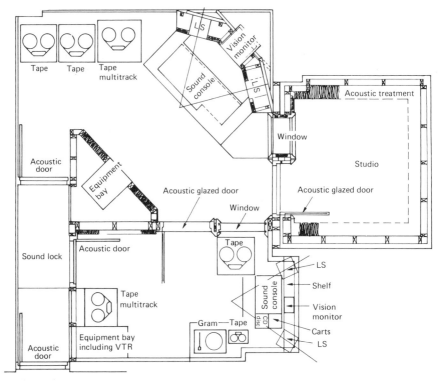

A small audio post-production video suite designed for mixing television programmes made in stereo with a separate mixing and track laying area

acoustic, and not just correct at some mid-reference point. It is not unusual for a room to have a short reverberation time (RT60) at high frequencies, but a longer one at low frequencies. This will, among other problems, produce an inaccurate stereo image. High-frequency reverberation can be treated with simple surface treatments. However, low-frequency problems often require changes in structural design.

After an area has been acoustically treated and the furnishings, equipment and speakers mounted, it is usual to take frequency response measurements in order to check the acoustics in the room. If problems do arise it is possible to electrically equalize the monitoring system, by modifying the frequency response of the speakers, to produce the desired acoustic response. However, this technique will not remedy, for example, deep notches in the frequency response, poor sound diffusion and poor stereo imaging. The electrical equalization of monitoring systems in small studios is not necessarily therefore an answer to acoustic problems. It may well appear to produce an improvement at one point in a small room, but at other positions in the room problems may well be exaggerated. However, these techniques can be used satisfactorily in large environments such as cinemas.

Background noise

It is important that the audio post-production studio environment is quiet. Additional noise is distracting and can affect the ability of the sound mixer to hear accurately, although when mixing mono material, it is reasonably easy to ignore background noise as the brain tends to eliminate sounds not originating in the monitoring speaker. With stereo, however, background noise becomes more disturbing and it is difficult to ignore the distractions of ambient sound within a room (such as video cassette recorders with spinning heads and fans, buzzing power transformers, video monitors, air-conditioning, and passing traffic).

To assess how distracting external noise can be, architects use noise contour curves (NC curves). Measurements of the acoustic noise of a room are made, using special octave wide filters. The NC rating is weighted to allow higher levels of noise at low frequencies, matching the sensitivity of the ear. A noise level of NC25 is a practical and acceptable level, making it just possible to hear fingers rubbing together with arms at the side. (Figures between NC5 and NC10 are considered very good.) To achieve a suitable figure, noisy equipment should be removed from the monitoring environment.

The importance of listening levels

When mixing any type of programme material, it is important to monitor it at the correct volume. This will be determined by the level at which the material will eventually be reproduced. There is a strong temptation in the sound studio to monitor at high levels, so as to produce an apparently finer and more impressive sound. However, since the ear's frequency response is not flat, but varies considerably with listening levels, the temptation should be resisted. While very loud monitoring levels tend to assist in discovering technical problems and aid concentration, they will not assist in creating a good sound balance. It is all too easy to turn up the monitoring levels while being enthusiastic and enjoying a programme, forgetting the problems this will create. Once the sound level is set at the start of a mix, it should never be altered; it should be set to a normal reproducing level.

The requirements for film audio post-production monitoring rooms are set out in the American National Standards Institute and the Society of Motion picture and Television Engineers' publication ANSI/SMPTE 214/1984 and are widely accepted as an international standard. A sound pressure level of 85 db has been adopted which is recommended to be 6 db below the level at which an optical soundtrack will clip.

Television monitoring conditions

The ANSI/SMPTE 212M television control room recommendations are to be treated with more caution. They recommend a monitoring system with a response rolling of at 1.5 db per octave above at 2 kHz. There is also a bass roll-off of 6 db/octave below 100 hz. This does not entirely reflect the

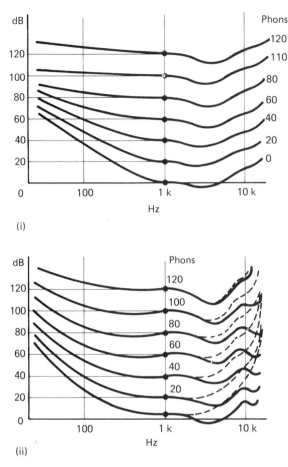

(i)

(ii)

Equal loudness curves demonstrating that the ear is more sensitive to changes in volume at middle and high frequencies; (i) Fletcher Munsen curves; (ii) Robinson and Dadson curves include the age of the listener, unbroken line a 20 year old; broken line 60 year old.

frequency response of equipment in many high-quality domestic environments. The SMPTE figures are perhaps more suitable for worse case checking.

A television monitoring environment should try to simulate the listening conditions of the average living room. In Britain this size is likely to be about 5 × 6 × 2.5 metres, with the reverberation time having little dependency on frequency, (given average furnishings it being about 0.5 sec). Since the majority of television viewers live in cities where environmental noise is high, and sound insulation poor, there is likely to be a high level of distracting noise. This is countered by turning up the volume, although consideration for the neighbours will restrict this – giving a sound volume range available of about 35 db in the worst case. An appropriate listening level in the home is likely to fall between 75 and 78 db (compared to 85 db in the cinema).

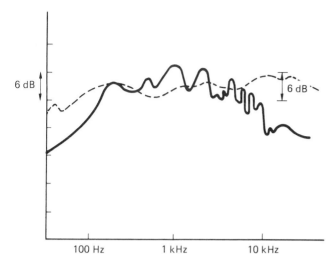

(i) —— The audio response of a good quality stereo television receiver; (ii) ---- The audio response of a studio monitoring loudspeaker

Television control rooms designed for stereo sound monitoring are likely to have:

1. Nearfield sound monitoring with viewing by video monitor.
2. Speakers placed at three widths apart on either side of the screen.
3. Speakers subtending an angle of 60 degrees.
4. Facilities to check mixes on high-quality and poor-quality speakers.
5. A reverberation time of less than 0.5 sec.
6. The operator closer to the loudspeakers than the surrounding wall.
7. A listening level set to about 75 db SPL.

The introduction of high-definition television with its wide screen formats (in enhanced C-MAC this gives a ratio of 1.65 to 1) will increase the effectiveness of stereo sound.

Film theatre monitoring conditions

At least three loudspeakers are used to reproduce the stereo sound image across the motion picture cinema screen, designated left, centre and right. In addition there is a surround channel within the theatre itself. Usually, four channels of sound are encoded, onto only two recording channels, via a matrix.

Through the matrix, the information on the left is fed directly to left track. The information on the right is fed directly to the right track. The centre is fed at a reduced level to both in phase. The surround is fed at a reduced level to both, out of phase, and has a delay line in its output.

Matrixed systems are not cross-talk free; this means sound from the screen speakers can be heard in the surround speakers. However, this effect can be all but eliminated by adding a delay line to the surround

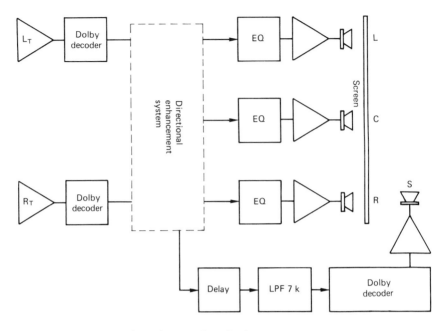

The Dolby stereo two track matrix system in replay form

speakers, and restricting the frequency response of the system to 7 kHz. The brain then identifies the first place from which a sound is heard as the sound's origin, and mentally ignores other sources of the same sound arriving a fraction of a second later. The signal from the front speaker reaches the ear first, so the mind ignores the same signal from the surround. (This is known as the Haas effect.) The position of the surround speakers is not critical, providing that there is a good balance between front and surround channels.

Reproduction of motion picture film on television

More and more motion picture feature films are now being distributed for home use; specifically mixed for reproduction in the cinema environment, these soundtracks may not be entirely suitable for domestic reproduction. In general a cinema mix when replayed in the home will have the music and effects at too a high a level. This means that the dialogue can become inaudible or unintelligible. In addition, dialogue equalization used in cinema film soundtracks to improve articulation and intelligibility, can reproduce as sibilance on high frequency transients giving the impression of distortion in the domestic environment.

These problems are compounded in domestic stereo situations for here, the reproducing environment is flat and narrow, with little reverberation, since the speakers are in a near-field environment. This is incompatible with the motion picture mixing theatre which offers a widespread image with more reverberation, and is a far-field recording environment. As such it is not particularly suitable for recording stereo sound for television. Any sounds of long duration, tend to sound louder in a film theatre than they really are. Therefore, sounds that are powerful in a loud scene in a mixing theatre, will sound somewhat less so at home. 'Mixing-up' is an answer. The stereo television sound is difficult to reproduce correctly in a motion picture mixing theatre, as the large distance between the two speakers means that there is, in effect, 'a hole in the middle' – which does not exist in the near-field environment.

From this, it can be seen that it is difficult to produce a good mix that will be entirely suitable for both the motion picture environment and the home environment. In an attempt to recreate the cinema experience in the home, surround decoders are available for use with encoded video cassettes.

Visual monitors

Loudspeakers in studios provide aural monitoring of the signal. To accurately record these sounds it is necessary to have a precise form of visual metering. These two forms of monitor, the loudspeakers and the meter, must be carefully matched. The average recording level must correspond to a comfortable, recommended, relevant monitoring level within the studio environment. Neither the monitoring volume nor the meter sensitivity should be changed if the sound level is to remain consistent. When mixing, it is usual for sound to be judged almost entirely from the monitoring systems, with only occasional reference to the metering, which provides a means of calibrating the ear. Two meters have been classically used for monitoring monophonic sound, and much is written about them in other books.

The VU meter

VU meters are constructed in virtually the same way as AC volt meters and measure the mean average or RMS voltage of a sound signal.

For over fifty years the VU meter has been the American standard for visual monitoring. If the signal is intermittent, such as speech, the VU meter will indicate an average value. This will be considerably lower than the instantaneous maximum levels that are found in the material. (To compensate this, engineers ride dialogue, perhaps 3 db to 5 db below the music.) The VU meter was never intended to indicate peak distortions, or to indicate noise. Its advantages are in its ability to monitor mixed programme material, giving an apparent indication of loudness (which peak meters will not). VU meters are now being produced with LED indicators to indicate when peaks are reached.

The main attraction of the VU meter is its price. It is inexpensive, being merely a calibrated volt meter. However, many units do not reach the standard recommendations required and are often too fast and too 'bouncy'.

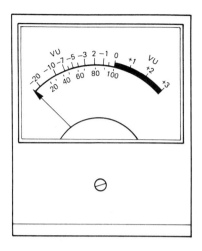

A VU meter (volume unit meter)

The peak programme meter

The peak programme meter (PPM) is not quite as old as the VU meter but its 40 year old standards are still in use. It is much favoured in Europe as it provides a more accurate assessment of overload, indicating programme peaks instead of their RMS value. It overcomes the short-comings of the VU meter by holding peak levels, but it gives no indication of loudness. Calibrated normally between 0 and 7, the PPM has a 4 db difference between each of the equally spaced gradations but 6 db between the gradations 0 and 1 and 1 and 2.

When peak signals occur they are held in the circuit, and other information is ignored. In order to read the meter it is therefore necessary to wait until the peak hold circuit decays. The peak programme meter is normally lined up to 8 db below the peak modulation point.

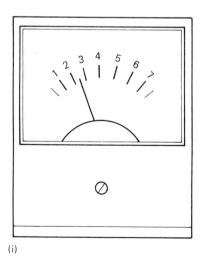

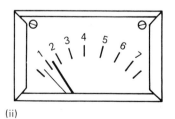

(i)   (ii)

(i) PPM (a peak programme meter); (ii) Stereo PPM (with two separate coloured meters)

Other types of displays

Traditionally, needle meters are used to visually monitor sound levels, but other forms are available, such as bar graph displays, which use light segments that can be illuminated to show level.

The colour of the display may change with high levels of modulation. Generally speaking, changes in levels and breaks in sound are easier to detect on this type of meter than on a needle meter. In addition, it is easier to see very low levels of sound on bar meters as they often show significant indications at 40 db below peak. In contrast, PPM, cannot show much below 25 db and the VU, much below 12 db.

Meter displays can be placed within video monitors but there are a number of drawbacks:

1. Visibility is very dependent on the content of the picture.
2. To reduce the complexity of the meters, some manufacturers do not include scale markings, and this can make these types of meter difficult to line up.
3. Because of the need for burnt-in time code in audio post-production, meters have to be placed at the sides of the screen. With time code information and meters, TV monitors can become very cluttered.

Mono and stereo metering

Stereo sound recording systems require meters, for each channel, with often an additional mono meter to monitor sound for the many monophonic systems that exist. It is normal to make visual meter and aural monitor checks by adding both signals together. In this situation, it might seem reasonable to expect the left and right signals to add up to roughly twice the value of left and right signals together. However, in practice, this increase in level will vary with the degree of correlation between the two

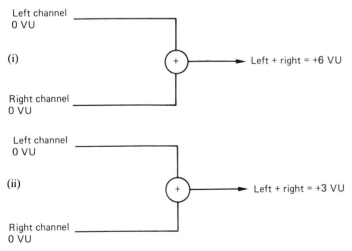

(i) Total correlation between left and right; (ii) No correlation between left and right

signals. If, for example, the two separate stereo signals were out of phase with each other, a combined mono signal would be less than either of the two individual signals. Only when the 'stereo' signals are identical, of equal amplitude, with 100% correlation such as a panned mono source in the centre of the sound field, equally divided between the two, will the combined signal be double that of the individual ones, (an increase of 6 db).

When there is no correlation between the channels, the sum level of equal amplitude signals is 3 db higher than either input channels. Therefore in a worse case situation there is a 3 db difference between mono and stereo audio of equal amplitude. Different organizations take different attitudes to the problem. In Britain the BBC uses a 3 db level drop (attenuation), for a combined mono signal, while NBC makes no attenuation at all. Much depends on the type of material being recorded, the recording techniques and the correlation. In practice the difference in sum level between mono and stereo falls somewhere between 0 and 3 db.

Phase metering

In right and left channel systems, 1 db of level difference between the left and right channels will be hardly detectable although a 3 or 4 db error will cause the stereo image to be slightly one-sided. This condition does not cause a major problem for stereo listeners but should the discrepancy be caused by phase errors between the two signals this can produce difficulties for mono listeners. Errors in phase are essentially errors in time between two sources, caused, for example, when a stereo replay head is misaligned at an angle to a standard tape. In this situation on replay audio on one track is heard fractionally before audio on the other. The different timing is expressed as an angle. The more complicated and longer the programme chain is, the more chance there is of phase problems building up in stereo.

	15°	30°	45°
Frequency (Hz)	[Loss (db)]		
1 000	0.00	0.00	−0.01
2 000	0.00	0.00	−0.02
5 000	−0.01	−0.06	−0.16
10 000	−0.06	−0.29	−0.68
12 500	−0.11	−0.46	−1.08
16 000	−0.18	−0.28	−1.83

Chart showing loss (db) at sample frequencies for a given phase error at 10 kHz

In analogue stereo recording, phase problems first build up with incorrect alignment of the heads. Film and multitrack systems can suffer particularly badly from head misalignments, since phase problems are critically affected by the distance between tracks (see page 123).

To ensure that phase problems can be quickly discovered, reference phase tones on tapes should be copied from recording to recording, rather than be regenerated at each stage. Programme material with mono information can be usefully used to confirm phase condition. Centre-located dialogue from a mono source, (having left and right signals of equal amplitude and in phase) is particularly useful in picking out phase errors.

Phase oscilloscope

The most straightforward and simplest way to display the phase relationships between two signals is to use an oscilloscope display. The left signal produces a vertical deflection, while the right signal has a horizontal deflection. When the signals are perfectly in phase, and of equal level, a line slanting 45 degrees to the right will appear. As the in-phase condition changes, ellipses will appear on the display.

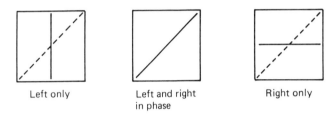

Left only   Left and right   Right only
                     in phase

Steady tones without phase error as seen on an oscilloscope

When the display shows a circle, there is a 90 degree phase difference between the two signals.

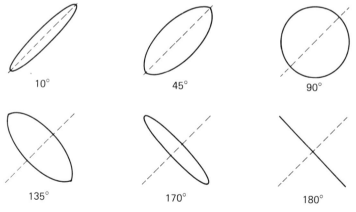

10°   45°   90°

135°   170°   180°

Steady tones with phase error

This type of meter not only shows the initial alignment of a stereo reproducer when playing back alignment tones, but it can also gives a continuous evaluation of phase during the recording. In the correct in-phase condition there is a narrow straight line of 45 degrees. The sound image is in the centre. Switching from stereo to mono means that the image does not move.

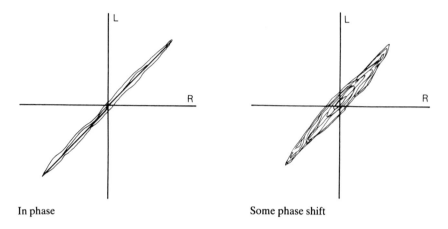

In phase   Some phase shift

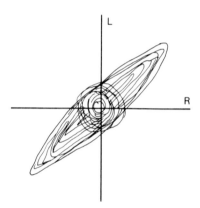

Increased phase shift

When there is a moderate amount of phase shift, switching between mono and stereo, produces a barely perceptible change in frequency content (a slightly enlarged line). This will be heard as a slight high-frequency roll-off. The high frequencies will be more out of phase than low frequencies if the fault is due to azimuth head misalignment.

Further shifts in phase cause a circular pattern in the centre of the display. This could be derived from voice sibilance. If the sibilance is out of phase between the two sources in the mid to high frequencies range, it will move to either side of the sound field, away from the main dialogue position.

An out-of-phase relationship of 30 degrees is undetectable at 10 kHz, and since most material generally passes though a number of generations before release or transmission, a 15 degree out of channel phase relationship is often recommended as the maximum per generation at 10 k. This leaves an additional 15 degree margin for errors during for transmission.

Scope graticule

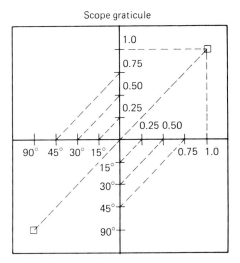

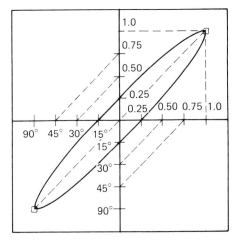

A graticule for covering the front of an oscilloscope to measure phase errors in stereo programmes, with an example of a 15° error between the channels

16

Mixing consoles and audio processing equipment

In the audio post-production studio the mixing console is the main working area and the heart of the sound system. It is positioned to allow the mixer to hear the best sound, to view the picture comfortably, and to have good access to the various devices he needs to use during the mix.

In the film studio the mixer does not require access to the projector or to the film sound machines, and so they are usually positioned in a room close to, but away from, the mixing environment.

In video post-production, much of the audio equipment is needed during the track-laying or mixing process so it is impractical to place it anywhere but within the reach of the operator. Since most of the equipment is quiet in operation it is unnecessary to place it in a different environment. The video recorder may well, however, be noisy because of its spinning head and the use of cooling fans, so this is often placed in a separate room. Once the VCR has been loaded, it is unnecessary to touch it and there is no disadvantage in having it away from the sound control room. The multitrack tape recorder can also be positioned away from the control room, although access may occasionally be needed during a mix to perhaps spot erase part of a track. Other machinery in the audio post-production suite, such as turntables, CD players, and additional equipment needs to be at close hand to the mixing console. Such equipment is called outboard equipment, equipment within the console being known as inboard.

The mixing console

Essentially the mixing console is a device for collecting together various sound sources, processing them, and producing a composite output for the recording machine. This output may be in mono, two track stereo, or even four or six track stereo, for motion picture release.

In audio post-production the sound mixer's time is spent in viewing the pictures, and combining this with movement of the hand on the mixing desk, to produce the desired sound – it must be easy to translate 'thought from perception into action'.

Meters must be in line with the screen or on the screen, so they can be quickly viewed; similarly, all the controls should be close to hand and easy

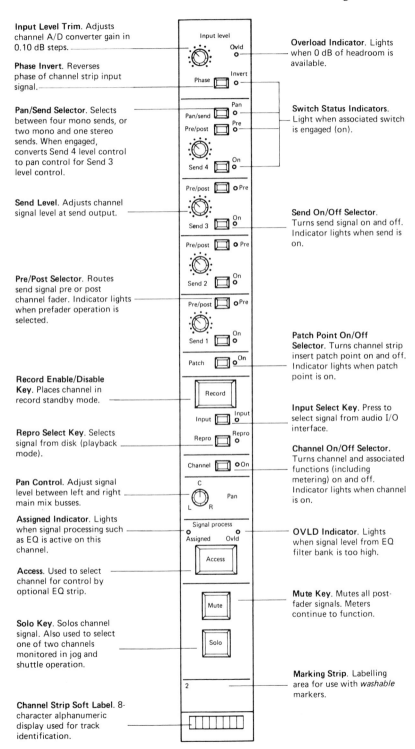

Input Level Trim. Adjusts channel A/D converter gain in 0.10 dB steps.

Phase Invert. Reverses phase of channel strip input signal.

Pan/Send Selector. Selects between four mono sends, or two mono and one stereo sends. When engaged, converts Send 4 level control to pan control for Send 3 level control.

Send Level. Adjusts channel signal level at send output.

Pre/Post Selector. Routes send signal pre or post channel fader. Indicator lights when prefader operation is selected.

Record Enable/Disable Key. Places channel in record standby mode.

Repro Select Key. Selects signal from disk (playback mode).

Pan Control. Adjust signal level between left and right main mix busses.

Assigned Indicator. Lights when signal processing such as EQ is active on this channel.

Access. Used to select channel for control by optional EQ strip.

Solo Key. Solos channel signal. Also used to select one of two channels monitored in jog and shuttle operation.

Channel Strip Soft Label. 8-character alphanumeric display used for track identification.

Overload Indicator. Lights when 0 dB of headroom is available.

Switch Status Indicators. Light when associated switch is engaged (on).

Send On/Off Selector. Turns send signal on and off. Indicator lights when send is on.

Patch Point On/Off Selector. Turns channel strip insert patch point on and off. Indicator lights when patch point is on.

Input Select Key. Press to select signal from audio I/O interface.

Channel On/Off Selector. Turns channel and associated functions (including metering) on and off. Indicator lights when channel is on.

OVLD Indicator. Lights when signal level from EQ filter bank is too high.

Mute Key. Mutes all post-fader signals. Meters continue to function.

Marking Strip. Labelling area for use with *washable* markers.

Input level

Ovld

Phase   Invert

Pan/send   Pan

Pre/post   Pre

Send 4   On

Pre/post   Pre

Send 3   On

Pre/post   Pre

Send 2   On

Pre/post   Pre

Send 1   On

Patch   On

Record

Input   Input

Repro   Repro

Channel   On

C
L   R   Pan

Signal process
Assigned   Ovld

Access

Mute

Solo

2

A channel strip on a digital console (*Courtesy of F W O Bauch Limited and Lexicon Opus*)

to find, without having to glance down, away from the screen, where action and sound are being related.

In designing consoles, it is important that the manufacturer makes them neither too small to be difficult to use, nor so large so that they take up too much space. A compromise must be reached and this can be difficult. Small controls increase the time taken to make accurate settings, (it has

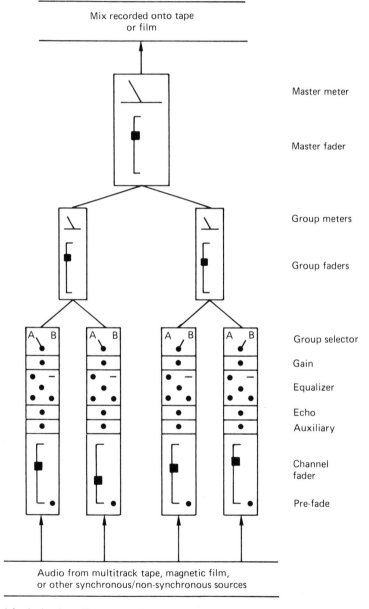

Mix recorded onto tape
or film

Master meter

Master fader

Group meters

Group faders

Group selector

Gain

Equalizer

Echo
Auxiliary

Channel
fader

Pre-fade

Audio from multitrack tape, magnetic film,
or other synchronous/non-synchronous sources

A basic simple audio console of modular design with two groups into a mono output been demonstrated that a control knob of two inches in diameter is the ideal size for operation); large controls make consoles so big that it is necessary to have 'extended' arms to use them. The length of consoles can be reasonably easily controlled; but it is the back-to-front distance that is the particular problem. This is where the main controls of the desk are to be found. Each sound source has its own fader to control the volume; further controls adapt the incoming sound by changing the audio frequency response and by sending the sound to special effect sources. Many of the sound channels, or input modules, will be similar. An optimum width for each strip is reckoned to be 40 mm, allowing the hands to cover five faders with comparative ease.

The number of input channels required for an audio post-production console depend on its purpose. In a small multitrack operation, perhaps using an eight track recorder, only twelve channels may be necessary. In a motion picture theatre where three people are operating the desk, 70 or 80 channels may be required.

Types of console

Two types of consoles are used in audio post-production, simple consoles feeding straight into recorders such as film mixing consoles, and consoles with more complicated monitoring facilities such as those used in multitrack/video post-production systems. In the latter it is necessary to replay already recorded audio tracks while still recording others. These types of consoles are manufactured in split console and in-line console form.

Split consoles

Split consoles have their sound monitor controls positioned together as a particular function of the desk. Usually these are to be found above the output faders.

In-line consoles

In-line consoles use what are known as in–out modules. These contain both channel controls and the monitor controls. The audio signal is sent to a specific track on the multitrack for recording, and this track is returned on playback to the same channel. Obviously, this takes up less space than the split console design but it does add more controls to the channel module. These types of desks are regularly used in the music recording industry and are often found in audio post-production work.

However, they provided more facilities than are often needed, for unlike music recording, where a large proportion of the tracks may be recorded at once (or a large number of microphone inputs routed to a few tracks), in audio post-production, sounds tend to be merely sent to one or two specific tracks. Completely flexible channel to track switching allowing any module to be sent to any track of the multitrack is unnecessary, and can be replaced by group routing where sound is fed to a specific master control

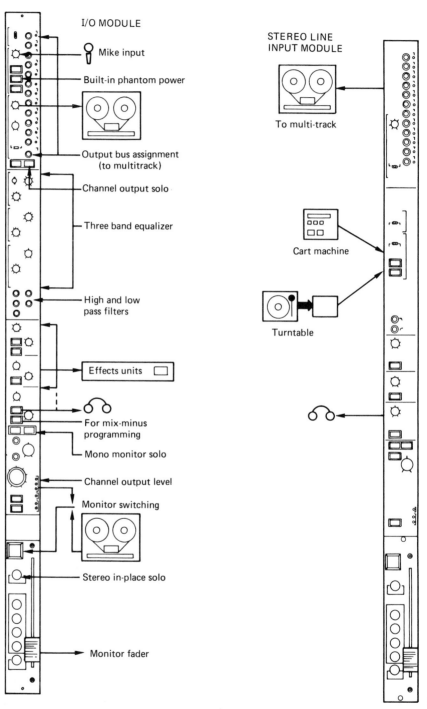

(i)

(i) An in/out module for a multitrack desk and tape recorder; (ii) Stereo input module with limited facilities designed for sources that are already equalized (*Courtesy of Sony Broadcast & Communications*)

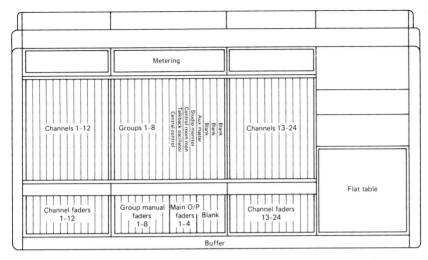

A 24 channel, 8 group console (*Courtesy of Neve Electronics International Limited*)

module. These groups, positioned at the centre of the desk, can then be dedicated to particular functions, such as music, effects and dialogue – and routed to the appropriate tracks.

Inputs and controls

Sound is delivered to a mixing console at microphone level and at a standard line level. In audio post-production consoles, there is only a limited requirement for microphone inputs. Most of the material comes from pre-recorded sources such as tape recordings, effects discs or sprocketed film reproducers.

The signal is first passed through a volume control or fader, to adjust the level of sound. In mono, this is simply routed to the desk's output, but in stereo, not only can the level be altered, but the sound can also be moved around the sound field. This movement is executed by means of a panoramic potentiometer – each channel having a 'pan' control which moves the sound image between the selected loudspeakers. In its simplest form the 'panpot' is a rotary control that moves the image across the two speakers. In a multitrack film mixing stereo system, a joy-stick allows the sound to be moved around the four- or six-channel sound field.

Other facilities available on the input channels include:

Auxiliaries

Each input module is likely to have various separate outputs (after the fader but prior to equalization) in addition to its normal outputs. These are called auxiliary outputs and are used to feed additional auxiliary equipment such as reverberation and delay units, as well as sending sound

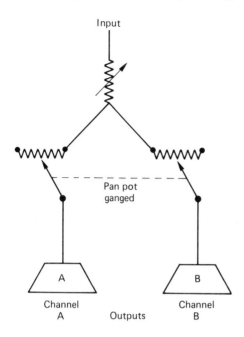

Input

Pan pot
ganged

A   B

Channel   Channel
A   Outputs   B   A panoramic potentiometer

to other sources solely for monitoring purposes. In post-synchronization, (the re-recording of poor quality location dialogue in a studio) it is necessary for the artiste to hear the original dialogue as a guide track; this can be sent via the auxiliaries (sometimes called foldback), to the artiste on headphones. Auxiliaries can also be used in less sophisticated consoles to monitor tracks already recorded whilst laying down other sounds during the track laying process.

Auxiliary returns

Some signals that are sent via the auxiliaries need to be returned to the console after, for example, the addition of echo. These processed sounds can be connected to an input channel or, alternatively, returned via a special auxiliary return, in the form of a stereo input, together with a level control, a pan control, and routing selection.

Audition

This is another form of auxiliary but one specifically for monitoring. It includes much of the audio chain; for example, reverberation and equalization.

M/S switches

M/S switches allow M + S matrix stereo format recordings to be processed within the desk itself. These are usually dialogue tracks.

Mutes

Mute switches are cut buttons that silence a channel and are often used to cut out background noise when audio signals are not present.

Phase reversal switches

Phase reversal switches merely reverse the phase of the input connector. They can provide quick confirmation that stereo is present.

Prefade listen (PFL)

Pressing the PFL button on a channel allows the channel to be heard before the fader is brought up. This can be used to advantage if tracks have unwanted sounds on them. These noises can be heard on PFL with the fader down and lifted when the problem has passed. (AFL is after fader listening).

Solo

This is similar to PFL but when operated, this mutes all other channels, making it particularly easy to hear the selected audio channel.

Width controls

Width controls give an apparent impression of greater width to the stereo image by feeding a certain amount of the material, out of phase back, into the channel.

Equalizers

Simple equalization consists of treble and bass controls for changing the frequency response of the sounds. Equalizers are invariably used in audio post-production to match sounds. They can also be used to give sound apparent distance or perspective; for example, as a performer walks away from a camera his voice will reduce in bass content. This effect can be re-created by careful use or equalization.

The equalization or 'eq.' can be made more sophisticated by offering more frequencies for adjustment, and by adding control of the width of the frequency band used. This is known as the Q. The Q frequency can be switchable to various selectable values, or it can be continuously adjustable with the variable centre frequency. In the latter form the equalizer is called a parametric equalizer.

In audio post-production, switchable equalization has advantages since it can be quickly and accurately repositioned during a mix to match a previous setting. The more complicated the equalizer, the more difficult it becomes to reproduce its position successfully. Audio post-production consoles tend to use simpler forms of equalization because of this, although with computer memories to aid mixing more complicated equalization is possible.

There was once a general philosophy in the broadcasting and music industries, that frequency response correction should only be used to correct the deficiencies of equipment, rather than to modify sound, so the term 'equalizer' was applied. This philosophy has changed, but even so equalization should only be used with caution. The ear only too easily becomes accustomed to a particular unnatural 'quality' of sound which it then considers to be the norm.

There are other forms of equalization found on sound consoles.

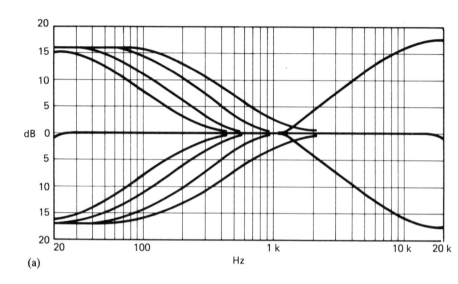

(a)

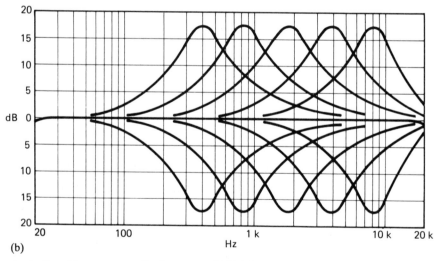

(b)

A selection of frequency equalization curves; (a) high frequency control with a 10 khz turn over with 18 db variable boost, and a low frequency control turn over at 33, 56 100 or 180 with 18 db boost or cut; (b) presence control peaking at 390, 820, 1.8 khz, 3.9 khz or 8.2 khz with 18 db variable cut or boost (*Courtesy of Neve Electronics International Limited*)

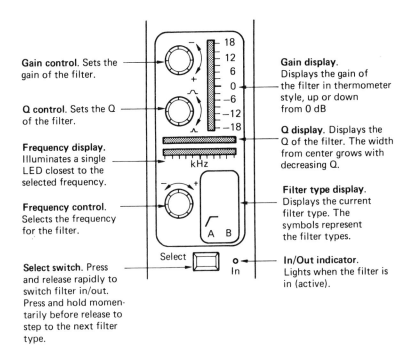

Gain control. Sets the gain of the filter.

Q control. Sets the Q of the filter.

Frequency display. Illuminates a single LED closest to the selected frequency.

Frequency control. Selects the frequency for the filter.

Select switch. Press and release rapidly to switch filter in/out. Press and hold momentarily before release to step to the next filter type.

Gain display. Displays the gain of the filter in thermometer style, up or down from 0 dB

Q display. Displays the Q of the filter. The width from center grows with decreasing Q.

Filter type display. Displays the current filter type. The symbols represent the filter types.

In/Out indicator. Lights when the filter is in (active).

Filter type	Symbol	Application
Parametric	⌁	Boost or cut can be set for a variable width frequency band centered around a selected frequency.
Notch	⋎	A very high Q (narrow band) filter with a very large (effectively infinite) cut value. The gain control is not used with this filter.
Hi shelf	⊏	Allows gain or cut to be set for all the region *above* the boundary frequency. The Q control is not used with this filter. 12 dB/octave.
Lo shelf	⊐	The Lo shelf is like the Hi shelf, except that the controllable region is *below* the boundary frequency.
Hi pass (Lo cut)	∫	A filter with a 12 dB/octave rolloff *below* the selected frequency. The Gain and Q controls are not used with this filter.
Lo pass (High cut)	⌐	Like the Hi pass, except the rolloff is above the selected frequency.

A frequency equalizer using bar graph meters and visual displays of the filter selected (*Courtesy of F W O Bauch Limited and Lexicon Opus*)

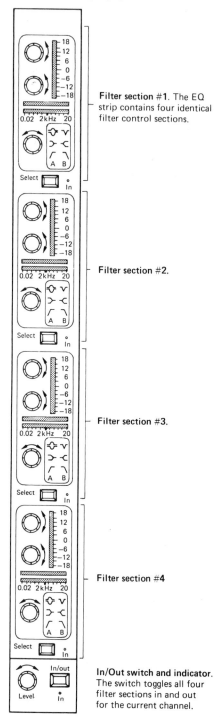

Filter section #1. The EQ strip contains four identical filter control sections.

Filter section #2.

Filter section #3.

Filter section #4

Level control. Sets the output level from the filter group. Levels are shown on the level display above the EQ strip. The left display shows the input and the right shows the output.

In/Out switch and indicator. The switch toggles all four filter sections in and out for the current channel.

An equalizer channel from a digital console (*Courtesy of F W O Bauch Limited and Lexicon Opus*)

Notch filters

Notch filters used in mixing consoles have a high Q and allow a specific frequency to be selected and attenuated. They are used to reduce such problems as camera noise and can be 'tuned' to the appropriate frequency. The offending noise can often be removed without completely destroying the basic sound quality. A depth of at least 20 decibels is necessary for successful noise rejection. Tuned to 50/60 hertz rejection, the filter can reduce mains frequency hum, with a further 100/120 hertz notch for its audible second harmonics. A 15 K notch filter can be used to reduce the 625 line sync pulse interference noise, radiating from domestic televisions in Europe.

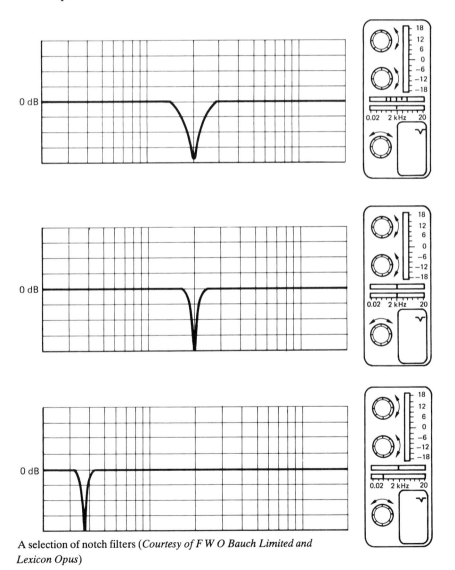

A selection of notch filters (*Courtesy of F W O Bauch Limited and Lexicon Opus*)

Pass filters

Low pass filters restrict the high-frequency response of a channel, allowing low frequencies to pass through. They are useful for reducing high-frequency electrical noise from fluorescent lamps, and motor systems as well as high-frequency hiss from recording systems.

High pass filters restrict the low-frequency spectrum of a system and permit high frequencies to pass. They are particularly useful in reducing low-frequency rumbles such as wind, traffic noise, and lighting generator noises.

Graphic equalizers

Graphic equalizers are able to provide equalizing facilities over the entire frequency range, and are often purchased separately from the console as outboard equipment.

They use sliding linear faders arranged side by side. This gives a graphical representation of the frequencies selected; hence the name, graphic equalizer. The individual filters are usually fixed and overlap.

They give quick and precise visual indications of the equalization used. As with most frequency response filters, graphic equalizers should be provided with a switch to remove the filter in and out of circuit, allowing the operator to check whether the effect being introduced is satisfactory.

Uses of equalizers

Equalization can be used for various reasons:

1. To match sounds in discontinuous shooting where the distance of the microphone to the performers varies as the camera shot changes; with equalization, it is possible to match the dialogue, producing a continuous cohesive sound quality.
2. To add clarity to a voice by increasing the mid-range frequencies.
3. To correct the deficiencies in a soundtrack if, for example, a voice has been recorded under clothing and is muffled.
4. To add aural perspective to a sound that has been recorded without perspective.
5. To remove additional unwanted sounds such as wind noise, interference on radio microphones etc.
6. To produce a special effect such as simulating a telephone conversation or a PA system.
7. To improve the quality of sound from poor quality sources such as transmission lines or archive material.
8. To improve sound effects by increasing their characteristic frequency for example, by adding low frequencies to gunshots or punches.

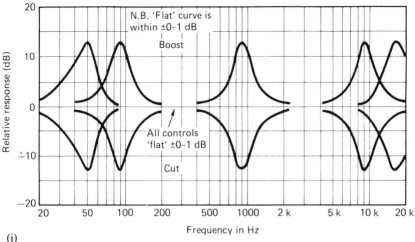

(i)

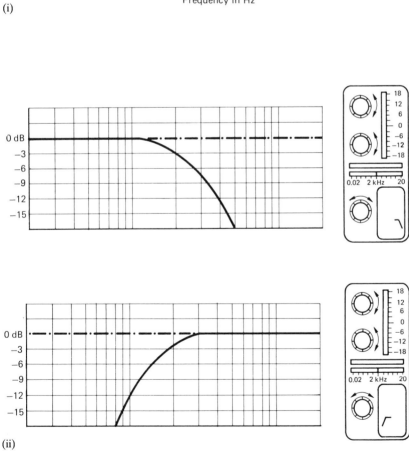

(ii)

(i) A graphic equalizer with selectable frequencies at 50, 90, 160, 300, 500, 900, 1.6 k, 3 k, 5 k, 9 k and 16 khz (*Courtesy of Klark-Technik Research Ltd*); (ii) low and high pass filters (*Courtesy of F W O Bauch Limited and Lexicon Opus*)

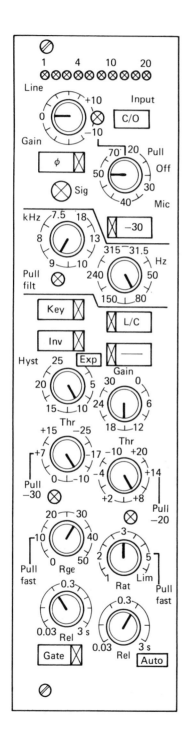

An analogue input amplifier. A gate/expander and limiter compressor is provided with a meter to indicate gain reduction. Hyst, hysteresis allowing greater control of the required signal to be compressed while still allowing the correct amount of signal through. Inv, inverts gate to ducker (*Courtesy of Neve Electronics International Limited*)

Control of dynamics

The range between high and low levels of sound, in reality, is often far greater than is needed for a sound mix. The simplest way to control this is to pull the fader down during loud passages, (where overload of the transmitter or the recorder could take place), and to push it up during quiet passages, (ensuring that sounds are not lost in the background noise of the system or the reproducing environment).

This manual dynamic control can work effectively, but it is often much simpler and easier to control dynamics automatically, using a compressor/limiter. More and more of these are being built into the channel modules of consoles, allowing each channel separate limiting and compression.

However, more normally they are found, and with greater sophistication, outside the console as 'outboard equipment'.

Limiting

Limiting is used to 'limit' or reduce a signal to a specific level. Further increases in input level results in no further increases in the output. The severity of the reduction is measured as a ratio, usually of 10 to 1; although some limiters can give ratios of 20, 30 or even 100 to 1 (the difference between these ratios is audibly not great). Some limiters may allow fast transients (that is, short fast rising signals) to pass through without being affected by limiting action. This maintains the characteristic of the sound without the limiting effect being audible.

Compression

Compression is a less severe form of limiting that is used to produce certain specific effects as well as to control and limit level. The onset of the limiting effect is smooth and progressive. The threshold point is the point at which compression starts, ratios being between 1.5 to 1 and 10.1

Low compression ratios operated at low threshold points will preserve the apparent dynamic range of programme material (despite compression). However, at the same time, they will allow a high recording level and thus give a better signal to noise ratio. A high ratio at a high threshold point, gives similar results but with the probability of a more noticeable limiting action.

The speed of the attack of incoming signals into a compressor or limiter is called the attack time. The quality of the compressed sound is very dependent on the speed at which the compressor attacks the incoming sounds. Slow attack times will result in a softening or easing of the sound. As the attack time lengthens more high frequencies will pass unattenuated through the system; on speech this will lead to sibilance. Slow attack times are useful when a considerable amount or compression is needed and, when used with a tight ratio, low frequency sounds will have maximum impact. With deliberate overshoot these sounds will have added punch, which can be useful in recording sound effects. Faster attack times are

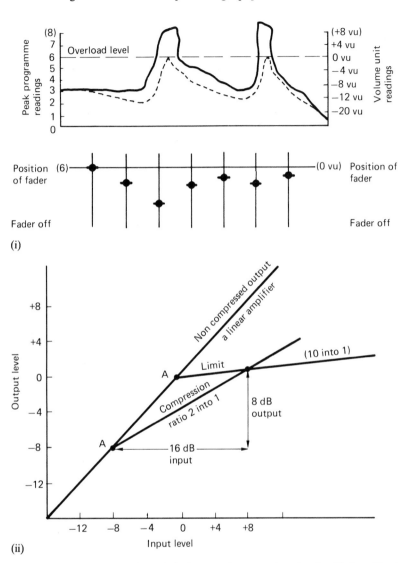

(i) Adjustments to a sliding linear fader in manual compression of audio; (ii) Sound level diagram showing the effects of limiting and compression, 'A' being the breakaway threshold point from the linear

necessary for speech and can be used to assist in controlling apparent loudness.

With very fast release and attack times and high ratios of compression, the low signal content of programme material is raised. This produces a subjective increase in loudness and is particularly useful, if carefully used, in increasing dialogue intelligibility. Unfortunately if an extremely fast release time is used, a pumping or breathing effect becomes apparent as the background level goes up and down in volume with the sound.

Recovery times can often be set automatically in compressors, being dependent on the level of the input signal. A specific recovery time is automatically programmed when the signal reaches above a certain threshold. As soon as the input falls below this threshold level, the recovery time smoothly changes to a shorter one, perhaps from ten seconds to one or two seconds. This is sometimes referred to as the 'gain riding platform'. It is used in some broadcasting transmitters where considerable overall long term compression is needed, and can affect the sound of carefully mixed programme material.

When compression is used on an entire mix, it is possible to end up with one dominant signal on the track. This can be a particular problem when using loud sound effects, or music under dialogue, and may even show itself as pumping or breathing. It is therefore, better to compress the various sections of the mix separately, rather than all at once. Effects and music under dialogue can even be held down with a compressor, rather than with a fader.

Certain compressors are capable of splitting compression into various frequency bands, and this can be particularly useful with dialogue where the power varies at different frequencies and unnatural effects can be reproduced. These occur at the lower end of the frequency components of speech that form the body of words, and give character.

Normally compressors incorporate gain level controls allowing levels to be maintained even when gain reduction takes place. In this way a direct comparison can be made between the compressed and the uncompressed material.

Noise gates and expanders

Noise gates and expanders are the inverse of limiters and compressors. A compressor is used to reduce dynamic range, whereas a noise gate is used to increase dynamic range by reducing the quieter passages further. The point where the reduction in level occurs is called the 'gating threshold', and this is adjusted to just above the unwanted sounds.

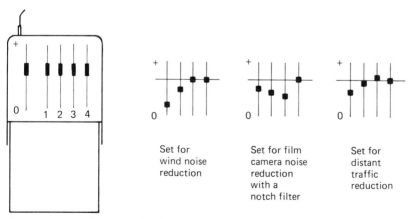

A frequency selective noise reduction device operating at four frequency bands

Normally inserted at the input to the channel, noise gates must be used with care, since low-level sounds, such as whispered dialogue that are required for a mix, can be treated as unwanted noise and also reduced in level.

Some noise gates are available as frequency selective devices, so that each band of the frequency spectrum can be individually noise-gated. This is ideal for reducing camera noise, and other unwanted sounds, recorded on location. The attack times and release times of the gate must be as short as possible, to minimize clipping on programme material. Expansion can also be used as a method of noise suppression, by exaggerating the difference between the wanted and unwanted sounds.

Limiters and compressors are used to:

1. Provide overload protection against over-saturating in the recording medium, particularly in digital or optical recording and when using metal analogue magnetic tapes, where over-saturation leads to instant unacceptable clipping.
2. Reduce the dynamic range of material to make it more suitable for the final format, (non hi-fi video cassettes and 16 mm optical sound films, have a very limited dynamic range).
3. Automatically reduce the range of sound to a comfortable level, for domestic consumption.
4. Increase the apparent loudness or create impact.
5. Increase the intelligibility of speech and the 'definition' of sound effects.
6. In noise gate and expander form, reduce to background noise levels.

Reverberation

Other facilities provided on the console include units designed to add artificial reverberation. Reverberation occurs when sound waves are reflected off surfaces – this is not the same as echo, which is a single reflection of a sound. Reverberation adds colour, character and interest to sound and sometimes even intelligibility. Reverberation accompanies nearly all the sounds that we hear, and its re-creation can be a very vital part of a sound mix, particularly in speech, when quite often sound that is totally lacking in reverberation seems unnatural. Natural reverberation helps to tell the ears the direction that sound is coming from, the type of environment that the sound was recorded in, and approximately how far away it is. It is particularly relevant in stereo recording.

Clapping the hands gives an excellent indication as to the reverberation of an environment, and one often used by sound recordists when they first encounter a new location.

When the hands are clapped, sound radiates in all directions at a rate of about a foot per millisecond. The first sounds to reach the ears come directly from the hands, and tell the brain where the sound source is. The next sounds heard come from early reflections, and these will be slightly different from the original sound waves since some of this sound energy will have been absorbed by the surfaces that the sounds have struck, (this absorption will depend on frequency). These early reflections can extend

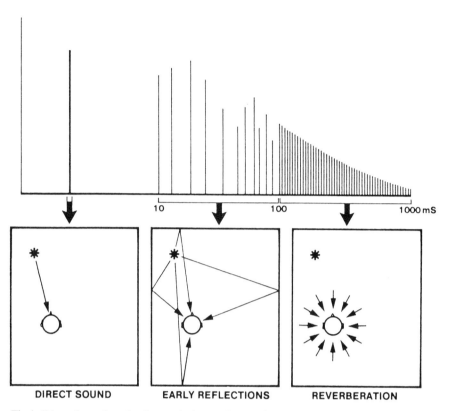

The build up of reverberation from a single sound source (*Courtesy of Klark-Teknik Research Ltd*)

from 5 ms, up to about 200 ms in a large hall. These reflections will build up quickly to an extremely dense sound, coming from all directions – no longer from just the hands. The ears now receive a slightly different pattern of reflections, at different times, from different directions. The time this effect takes to die away is called the reverberation period.

If an electronic device is to re-create reverberation satisfactorily it must take into account all these parameters.

Essentially, reverberation units take sound and delay it – often through digital delay lines. These delays can range from a few tens of milliseconds, to a few seconds. The re-creation of the acoustic of a small room requires only a few milliseconds of delay, whereas a few seconds of delay is required to re-create a public address system. By taking different parts of a digital delay line and applying degrees of feed-back and filtering, more sophisticated effects can be created. It is possible to de-tune the delay and with time slippage, to produce an effect that will split mono sound into pseudo stereo. Perhaps, more useful in audio post-production are pitch-changing and time-compression devices, where specific sounds can be made to fill predetermined time slots. An example might be where an additional piece of dialogue has to be added to an edited picture, or where a voice-over for a commercial is too long and needs to be shortened. Using a delay device this sound can be fed into a memory and then read out at a different speed, either faster or slower, but at the same pitch. Reading out data slower than it is fed in, means that the system has to repeat itself and there may be an audible hiccup or 'glitch' in sound.

Computerization of mixing consoles

The vast complexity of modern recording consoles has led manufacturers to provide computerized aids to mixing, making it possible to memorize every setting at a particular point in a mix.

Console automation should never hamper the creativity of the mixer. In the ideal system, the operator would need to use no extra controls. Unfortunately this is not possible, but it is possible to go a long way towards this goal, much depending on the type of memory storage used and, whether it be a reset or a recall system.

Recall merely tells the operator where the controls should be, but it does not reset them to the positions. Recall information is usually in the form of a video display unit, indicating where, for example, equalizers should be placed to corrrectly reproduce their positions. Re-set, however, remembers positions and puts the controls physically back to their memorized points.

A computerized mix can either be memorized on a floppy disc, or recorded as digital information on the audio track of a tape recorder used in the system. In the latter, however, the automation is only accurate when the tape is running at speed. The accuracy of automation is not vitally important in mono, since each individual sound source is controlled independently. However, in stereo the situation is different, for it is vital that a stereo pair of controls move together or else the stereo image will move across and around the sound field as mis-tracking takes place.

Automation is particularly useful in audio post-production. A total automation system, for example, can memorize all the manipulations available on a console for later reference. But these systems are extremely complex, since many larger consoles have 6 000 or more functions. To meet these memory requirements, the computer processor must be capable of dealing with up to a thousand million instructions per second – compared with a typical personal computer, which is capable of handling about a million instructions a second. Simple fader-only automation systems require 40 or 50 times less power.

It is vital that any automation system is capable of resetting all the necessary information within the time it takes for the audio recorders and the video machine to reach synchronization. A system is of little use if the picture and soundtracks are up to speed and running in lock, but the automation system is still trying to synchronize.

The high cost of total automation systems, means that they are found in very few analogue consoles. However digital audio consoles, are inherently programmable by their very design. Indeed, there is absolutely no reason why the whole sound automation and processing system in a digital console

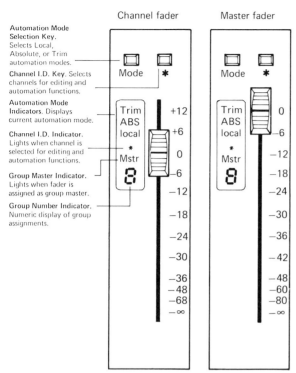

An automated channel fader as used on a workstation (*Courtesy F W O Bauch Limited and Lexicon Opus*)

should not be controlled from a single computer keyboard with a video display unit, and this is offered in some workstation designs.

Many automation systems are designed complete with controllers for the audio post-production suite, these provide the usual synchronizing facilities and controls.

17

The mix

Audio post-production of a programme is completed with the mixing of the soundtracks. The tracks will have already been prepared, either in the form of sprocketed magnetic films with spacer, or in the form of soundtracks built up on a multitrack tape recorder or on a computer disc. In the latter case, some of the tracks may have been already mixed and their levels set; much will depend on the time allocated, the equipment available and the experience of the mixer. The mixing process is the same whatever method is used.

There are both aesthetic and technical aspects to sound mixing. Technically, the most important part of audio post-production is to produce a match of the sound to the visuals so that sound appears to come from the pictures. The visual and aural perspective must be right – if an actor moves towards the camera it should sound as though he is moving towards the camera. If an explosion occurs half a mile away, it should sound as though it occurs half a mile away, regardless of how close it was originally recorded. Of course, all rules are there to be broken.

Aesthetically, audio post-production is concerned with mixing the various soundtracks to produce a cohesive, pleasing, dramatic whole, that enhances the pictures to the Director's wishes. A scene is more than just one sound following another (as are the visual pictures), it consists of sounds that knit whole scenes together, adding atmosphere and drama. Sound places pictures in geographical locations and indicates time. Unfortunately, sound is often considered very much a Cinderella compared to vision, and directors sometimes take little trouble to supervize mixing. Others, will take sound into account from the very start of a production.

Operation of the controller

During the mix, the soundtracks and the picture are controlled from the synchronizing controller. Originally in the 1930s, audio post-production systems in films were only capable of running in synchronization from stand still up to speed and into play. Once a mix had started the 'take' had to continue for the length of the roll to a maximum of 12 minutes. If a mistake was made, it was necessary to unlace, rewind the soundtracks and return to the beginning of the film for a new mix, or alternatively, to re-record the faulty sequence and cut it into the final mix. A successful mix was called a print, (since it could only be reproduced via a photographic print from the optical negative) and this term is still used today in the film industry. With the advent of magnetic recording, it became possible to replay the sound immediately rather than have to wait for a print to be photographically made. Originally these systems only ran at single speed, but they were later developed to run in interlock backwards and forwards at single and fast speeds.

The system is known as 'rock and roll', and is used in all audio post-production suites. The machines run forward; a mistake is made; the system is run back; it is then run forward again; recording begins at an appropriate point before the mistake. To make sure that the insertion into 'record' before the mistake, matches the previous recording, a balancing key or send/return switch is used. This compares the sound that is about to be recorded (the send), with the previously-recorded sound (the return). If, with the tracks running, the sound that is about to be recorded matches, (balances) sound that is already on the track, when the record button is pressed or 'punched in' there will be complete continuity of sound on the final master. This facility needs to be specifically designed as part of a monitoring system. However, on a standard multitrack mixing console 'send' and 'return' switching is often provided as part of the monitoring system itself.

Mixing, using 'rock and roll' techniques, can limit the continuity of a mix. The system is stopped and started every time a mistake is made – rehearsals can reduce these problems, but all this takes up time.

Pre-read displays

To assist the mixer in taking cues pre-read displays are sometimes used. These give visual warning that tracks are about to appear at the faders. On the machine replaying the soundtracks, a special head is fitted upstream of the actual replay head. This triggers a series of lights when a sound modulation is received. The lights stream across the screen or monitor, completing their path when the sound is appearing at the fader.

Pre-read systems can also operate without a pre-read head, (they are physically difficult to fit on multitrack tape recorders) by using a memory store device. During the first pass of a tape, (such as a lay-off), the modulations on the tape are memorized against time code. On replay for mixing, the stored modulation information activates the moving light display now operating in advance of the real time code, and pre-reading the sound.

Console automation

With the introduction of console automation, it has become possible for mixes to be memorized. The most basic form of mixing desk automation is

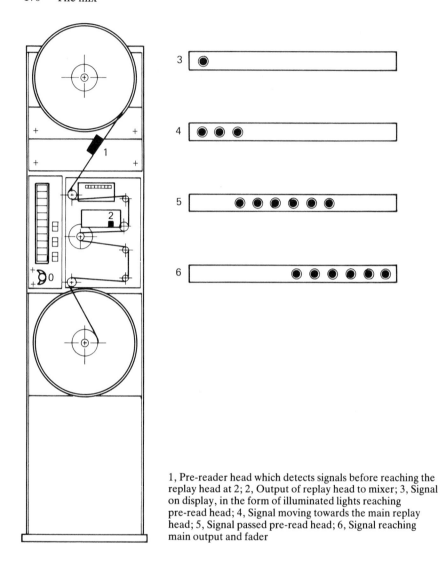

1, Pre-reader head which detects signals before reaching the replay head at 2; 2, Output of replay head to mixer; 3, Signal on display, in the form of illuminated lights reaching pre-read head; 4, Signal moving towards the main replay head; 5, Signal passed pre-read head; 6, Signal reaching main output and fader

the computer control of faders. This can be either in reset or recall form. In reset the faders physically move to their position. In recall 'tally' lamps indicate when a fader has been manually moved to its previously stored level. Channel mutes are often memorized as well as the fader position.

In the computer mix, the movement of the faders is memorized in exact synchronization with the soundtrack. On replaying such a mix, the operator is free to make updates. He merely overrides the movements of the faders where necessary, and makes a series of improvements to the mix until he reaches the final desired result. No longer is it necessary to stop a mix when a mistake is made, and lose continuity. The mixer now merely returns to the faulty part of the mix and just updates the memory.

Sound sources for the final mix

In a large audio post-production mix, such as a cinema feature film, seventy or more individual tracks may be used to make up the final soundtrack. In a small video production there may only be two tracks available, recorded on an industrial video recorder. Soundtracks for the final mix will have been provided from various sources:

1. Original dialogue that was recorded in the field, which may be in mono or stereo, and will also contain some incidental effects as well as the spoken lines.
2. Wildtrack dialogue that was also recorded in the field, not at the time of the shooting but immediately afterwards, and which has been fitted to the picture.
3. Post-synchronous dialogue which consists of dialogue which had been recorded to picture after the shoot.
4. Post-synchronous effects which were recorded in the studio and not in the field (foley effects). (See page 181.)
5. Effects which come from an effects library or location tapes.
6. Scored music that was especially composed and recorded to go with the production.
7. Source music which is intended to come from musical sources on or off the screen.
8. Library music that has been taken from a music library and matched to the pictures.

To assist the mixer take accurate cues during the mix, cue sheets are usually provided showing the various available sounds in graphical form. These may be prepared on paper or even on a video display unit.

Cue sheets

The sheet is divided into several columns, (up and down or across) depending on the number of soundtracks that have been prepared. Each soundtrack has its own column with the first column giving visual cues and timing. The columns may be sub-grouped into dialogue, music and effects. As the mix progresses, the tracks are identified against the time readings on the chart. The time counter within or below the picture provides film feet or time information tied to the picture, be it film or video.

The various soundtracks are mixed together with sounds cutting from one track to another, fading out and fading in or, alternatively, cross-mixing. Equalization, reverberations, compression and limiting are added as required.

Pre-mixes

If a large number of tracks are being mixed together, they may need to be sub-grouped into various smaller mixes, for easier handling. In film, the pre-mix will be recorded on a roll of magnetic film, for later playing off a

Audio mixing chart   Airport documentary

Time in seconds

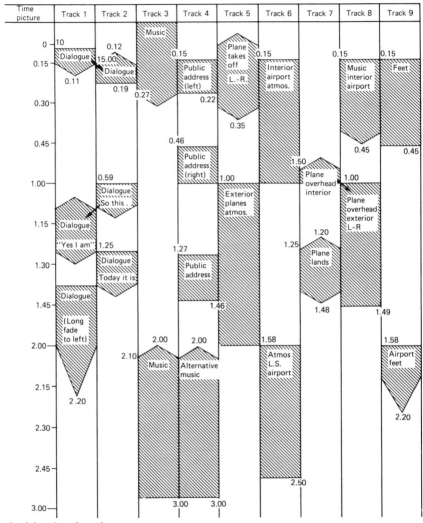

Time picture	Track 1	Track 2	Track 3	Track 4	Track 5	Track 6	Track 7	Track 8	Track 9

A mixing chart for a documentary

replay machine with other tracks. In multitrack operations it will be recorded onto one of the tracks of the multitrack machine.

Pre-mixes can be divided down into groups such as dialogue, effects and music; or, even further, into pre-mixes of spot effects, foley effects, atmosphere effects etc. Pre-mixes must be carefully handled, since it is possible for certain sounds to be obscured when the various pre-mixes are finally mixed together. Depending on the equipment, it may be possible to monitor other tracks while pre-mix recording takes place.

In many audio post-productions, the dialogue will be the most important part of the mix. A dialogue pre-mix is therefore often recorded first. This allows the mixer to produce the best possible dialogue quality, concentrating specifically on matching sound levels, frequency equalization and stereo positioning. The pre-mix may include panning information for stereo and possibly reverberation, but as many options as possible should be left open for the final mix.

When pre-mixing it is often sensible to occasionally reduce the studio monitoring level to confirm that the pre-mixed sounds will not be lost when added to the final mix at a lower level.

This can be a particular problem when heavy effects are being mixed under what will eventually be dialogue. Equal loudness curves demonstrate that we perceive sounds differently at varying levels, so any pre-mix must be treated with care.

Once the premix is completed the final mixing begins. Premixes are, perhaps not so necessary if an automated console is used.

Using an automation system the mix for a documentary video programme on an airport might progress as follows:

Five or six various effects need to be mixed, plus dialogue tracks. In the first pass, the mixer feels that the background atmosphere mix is correct but the spot effects of the public address system are too loud, and that the plane passing overhead reaches its loudest point a little too late; perhaps the Director doesn't agree with him. On the second pass, an attempt is made to improve the public address effect further, but this time the dialogue is slightly obscured. On the third pass, a slight attempt is made to increase the level and improve the intelligibility of the dialogue by reducing the background effects. This, the Director likes. Now, all three attempts can be reviewed and compared by memory recall. It is decided that the final mix should consist of the atmos mix from the first pass, the dialogue mix from the second, with the additional effects coming from the third. Now the sound mixer merely selects the fader movements required from the computer, and the final mix is produced.

As the final mix is being recorded, any last minute updates of the balance can also be carried out. This automation system may or may not, include automation of the equalization and the dynamics – this may have to be carried out manually.

A second approach is to use sections from the various mixes. The first 30 seconds from mix 1 is used; the next 40 seconds from mix 3; the rest from mix 2; making the combined final track.

A third approach is to use the computer for pre-mixing. Various soundtracks are taken and mixed as a pre-mix, and then further tracks are added so building up a final track.

If a non-automated mixing console is used, the mix will progress more carefully; each scene or section will be mixed and agreed upon before the next portion of the soundtrack is mixed.

Timeshifts during a mix

As the mix progresses it may become necessary to change the 'time position' of a soundtrack. Perhaps a piece of commentary interferes with a sound effect, or perhaps the position of a sound effect is wrong in relation

A mixing cue sheet or chart with 15 tracks, footage/time cues not included

to the visuals. Using a sprocketed magnetic film system, it is merely necessary to offset the track on the particular machine in relation to the picture. Using a digital disc system, it is merely necessary to tell the workstation how many frames to move the sound backwards or forwards. With both these systems this is easily achieved, but with an audio post-production system using a multitrack tape recorder the situation is a little more difficult. Here each soundtrack has been recorded physically in synchronization with the other soundtracks on the tape. In order to time shift a track it is necessary to offlay the sound onto another recording medium, and then replay it with the time shift. This may be a time consuming process, and does introduce another generation of sound.

Compatible stereo mixes

If a stereo mix is to be reproduced in mono, slight compromises may have to be made to the stereo image to allow for good mono reproduction. Sound effects will often need to be slightly reduced in level, so that they do not appear to be too close in the mono image. In addition, different sounds at either side of the stereo image, which may be comprehensible in stereo, may not be in mono when the image is combined in the centre and may in fact, sound too loud. This is further complicated when stereo pre-mixes are combined with further stereo pre-mixes. Artificial reverberation must be carefully controlled too – spectacular effects in stereo can easily produce unintelligibility when combined with mono.

In a stereo matrix recording system it is important that the mix is heard through the matrix, to ensure there are no phase problems.

Lay-back

By using level control, frequency equalization, varying dynamics and reverberation, the mixer has produced a final soundtrack reaching the artistic and technical standards required. This final mix must be suitable for the environment in which it is to be reproduced – the home, the cinema, the office, etc. etc. It may have to be compatible for both stereo and mono reproduction.

In the film re-recording process, this soundtrack is physically separate from the picture. Later, for motion picture theatrical release, and for some television use, it may be finally 'married' to the picture in the form of an optical (or even a magnetic) print. In the video system, however, at some point the audio master soundtrack has to be 'laid-back' onto the video master tape for transmission. Obviously, if the programme has been mixed and recorded onto the original edited master, this lay-back is unnecessary. Normally, however, the soundtrack is kept on a separate tape from the picture, in the audio post-production area, and has to be married back to the master picture. The synchronization of the lay-back is time code controlled. Since both picture and master soundtrack have the same code, a simple lockup with an audio transfer is all that is needed. Even with work stations, lay-backs are necessary for if the mixes are held in the work stations they must be returned to the video or film format for final replay.

Music and effects tracks

Much of the material that is audio post-produced needs to be revoiced into other languages for sales to foreign countries – for this a special soundtrack is made up, called an M & E (Music and Effects) track. It is sold as a 'foreign version' to countries that wish to post-synchronize their own language onto the material. The M & E track consists of all music and effects tracks, as well as vocal effects tracks such as screams, whistles, and crowd reactions tracks – in fact, sounds which cannot be identified as specific to a particular country. The balance of the mix should be as faithful a re-creation of the original language version as is economically possible. To assist in making a music and effects track, the final mix itself may be divided into and recorded as three separate tracks of dialogue, music and effects. (A technique often used in 35 mm productions.)

In documentary material with dialogue and commentary, the music and effects track often include synchronous dialogue, but not commentary. This commentary will then be re-read in the appropriate foreign language, the synchronous dialogue being subtitled or 'voiced over'. This saves the expense of post synchronizing. Indeed, more and more foreign productions are now being sold with subtitles rather than post-synchronized dialogue. However, subtitles can often only summarize dialogue; particularly in fast wordy sequences. This means that the subtleties of the spoken word may be lost.

18

Studio recording

It is often necessary to record dialogue for audio post-production, either as a commentary (for a commercial or documentary) or alternatively, when re-voicing foreign language films or post-synchronizing dialogue of poor quality. Dialogue may be recorded within the mixing suite or theatre itself, although this is far from satisfactory, as the acoustics are not ideal and there can be extraneous noise. It is more sensible to use a separate studio which is part of the audio suite which can also be used for recording sound effects.

Ideally, a studio used for speech recording should not suffer from low frequency 'booming' and it should have little or no self-resonance. The acoustic damping must not only reduce high-frequency reverberation, but also low-frequency as well.

The room must be insulated completely from external noise, and be equipped with the necessary facilities, including a footgage or timing counter, talkback, foldback, a cuelight and a picture monitor or screen. In film operations the picture can be viewed either directly, or through a television monitor linked to an electronic camera on the projector. This may allow the studio to be separate from the mixing area.

Recording dialogue

Performers delivering dialogue should be encouraged to stand so that the chest and diaphragm are unrestricted. However, to stand for long periods can be physically arduous, and many performers prefer to compromise by using a high stool and a lectern. Some prefer to sit at a table, but this is not particularly satisfactory.

The quality of speech can be improved by equalizing the signal electronically through the recording console. Compression can raise average signal levels, thereby increasing intelligibility by reducing variations in level. A slow attack time is not advisable here, as there is a tendency for the high-frequency content of the sound to pass unattenuated which can lead to sibilance. Although equalizers specifically designed to reduce this are available, they are not particularly effective. Equalization can also help to correct over-emphasis of low frequencies occurring through close microphone techniques. A certain amount of mid-lift is often given to dialogue (between 2 and 6 kHz), to increase intelligibility, although this can again create sibilance if over used. Dialogue equalization is particularly useful when speech is to be replayed at high volume such as in a cinema auditorium.

Post-synchronization

An original dialogue track may contain some material that is unusable – perhaps there is too much reverberation, too much background noise, or a fault in the recording machine. When this occurs the dialogue can be replaced by a method known as post-synchronization.

The dialogue to be post-synchronized is divided into small sections of anything from two or three words to a sentence or two. These words and their appropriate pictures are then played back to the artiste in a studio. The artiste listens, and repeats the words in synchronization with the picture as he hears the original dialogue through his headphones. The words and pictures repeat themselves in the form of a regular loop; a cue appears just before the dialogue is about to start. The words to be spoken may be displayed below the screen, in synchronization with the picture, using a 'band machine'. The scene repeats itself until the actor has achieved satisfactory synchronization, and a recording has been made.

Loop method

Traditionally, using a film system, the sections to be revoiced are made into two continuous loops of picture and sound. In addition, a virgin loop of sound is loaded onto the recorder which runs in synchronization with the guide track sound and picture. A streamer, or wipe, is physically drawn onto the picture with a chinagraph pencil, to cue the performer to speak. This line moves across the screen over 2 or 3 seconds finishing at the start cue. When the actor has perfected his words, another set of loops are 'put up'.

This system has many drawbacks. Obviously it is tedious and time consuming work to make up loops, and in large looping sessions storing loops becomes a problem. In order to reduce lacing up times some systems use two sets of equipment. In the early 1960s the automatic dialogue replacement system was introduced to improve efficiency.

Automatic dialogue recording – ADR

In this system, loops are made electronically and not by physically cutting the material. This lends itself well to non-sprocketed systems where it is impossible to physically cut the material and to maintain synchronization. In the ADR system the recording and playback machines are given two points to shuttle between, and are programmed to produce a bleep just before the 'loop' is about to start. The controller can be set to shuttle

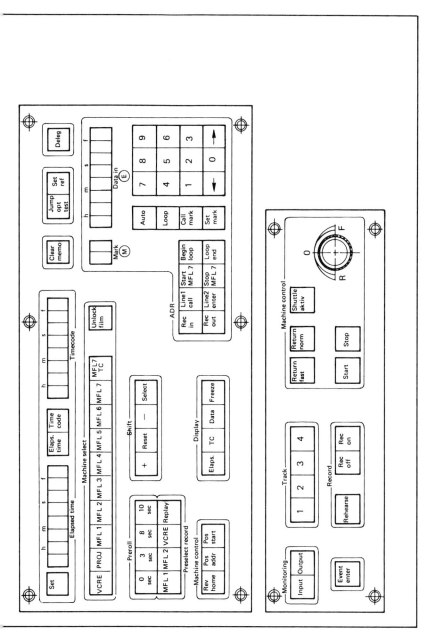

A film controller complete with an automatic dialogue replacement unit (*Courtesy F W O Bauch Limited and M W Albrecht*)

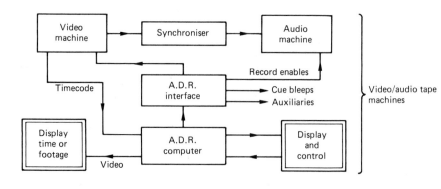

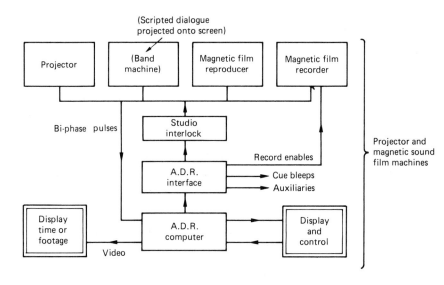

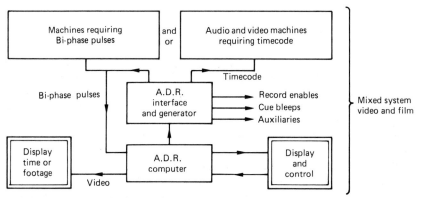

A selection of methods used in ADR with either video or film picture device (*Courtesy of Branch and Appleby Ltd*)

between any number of points, and after successfully completing one loop it automatically moves on to the next loop.

Automatic dialogue systems are offered on most video/audio post-production controllers. The number of recorded takes of each loop is equal to the number of tracks available on the machine. However, listening to ten or more takes of one particular loop is something of a daunting experience, making it very difficult to judge which is best.

The ADR system is well suited to digital disc recording, with their instant access and high-speed run-up. ADR originally met with some resistance, for it proved to be very fast, and actors and operators found that they no longer had time between loops to prepare themselves for recording the next one.

ADR can only be completely effective when all the material is held within one film reel or videotape. Some advantages of the system are lost if the operator is having to change from one reel to another to find the loop points. In large productions, this can be a problem. Since looping is not carried out in order, but is arranged around performers' availability, careful preparation is essential.

It is argued that post-syncing produces better performances from actors, since all their energies go towards giving a good verbal performance and they are not worried about remembering lines. But in looping there is no continuity of recording and little interplay with fellow actors. Scenes do not flow and it is difficult to obtain convincing performances in a sterile sound studio. ADR has a slight advantage over 'looping' since it allows actors to see performances either side of the shots to be looped.

Automatic dialogue replacement can be refined further by using an automatic time alignment system. This compares the relative timing difference between the post sync dialogue being recorded, and the original dialogue on the unusable track. The post-sync dialogue is automatically edited within the machine to match the original dialogue. The system normally runs 'hands free' but it is possible for the operator to adjust the parameters of the system to tighten the 'fit' of the dialogue.

Generally speaking, post-synchronized dialogue is recorded in dead acoustics, with the necessary equalization and reverberation being added in the final mix.

Post synchronous sound effects

When dialogue has been post-synchronized all the ambient sounds of the original track such as footsteps, doors opening and closing, clothes' rustles etc. are lost. However, these can be replaced, again by using post-synchronizing techniques (called Foley effects in the USA). Often, these additional effects are required even when original synchronous dialogue is used, for the incidental effects will be ignored in favour of the dialogue.

To reproduce sound effects in a studio the scene is first viewed, and the actions are then mimicked using similar props to the original scene. Unlike dialogue replacement, however, longer sections can be recorded at one time and guide tracks and loops are necessary. Usually footsteps, and clothes' rustles are recorded in this way. Spot effects however, are more difficult to synchronize accurately. Sometimes it is impossible to produce an exact sound effect from an actual prop because the real thing may not sound convincing; water spouting from a hose, for example, often sounds weak, but it can be transformed by adding the effect of a small waterfall. The sound of a large bird flapping its wings can be simulated with opening and closing an umbrella. Many contrived sounds are better than the real thing, and every possibility is worth investigating.

Soundtracks made specifically for foreign versions, will often require to be post-synchronized with effects and footsteps since the dialogue will have been removed, complete with all the other 'live' sounds.

Commentary recording

Not only are audio post-production studios used for post-synchronizing dialogue but they are also used for commentary recording. Commentaries or 'voice overs' can either be recorded before or after editing, but to assist the performer in giving the correct intonation it is better to record a commentary to the edited picture. To record a commentary without pictures, 'blind', may lead to a poor performance when later viewed against the visuals.

To prepare a commentary, a shot list giving footages or time is usually made. It will give details of the visuals, with cues for effects and music, and the in and out times for the synchronous dialogue. The commentary is then carefully written to the pictures taking into account the reading speed of the performer, which can be timed by counting a second for every three words spoken; or in film, two words for every 35 mm foot that passes, or 5 words for every 16 mm foot. Commentaries can be written to be informative or, alternatively, to be explanatory to the picture. Informative commentaries need the viewer to listen with attention; explanatory commentaries tend to merely accompany the picture with relevant words – they add to the production in an entertaining way and simply become part of the whole.

Once a commentary script is completed it is carefully marked with start and stop cues in the form of timings. In the studio, the commentator begins reading when the first time cue appears and attempts to finish by the out-cue. Through his headphones he will hear other relevant soundtracks which may provide valuable cue information – perhaps the commentary introduces a performer who speaks on a cue. An alternative to using time cues is to cue by use of a light.

The commentary script should be typed on only one side of the paper and laid out in front of the microphone so that it is unnecessary to turn pages. Should the commentator make a mistake in the middle of a narration, the recorded track can be run back and then rolled forward. The narrator will then hear his own voice through his headphones. He can judge the type of intonation he was using and at a convenient point, prior to the mistake, the track is switched from 'replay' to 'record' and the performer picks up the reading. If the intonation is correct, the insert will be imperceptible.

19

The transmission and reproduction of audio post-production material

Once audio post-production has been completed, the mixed soundtrack is ready for reproduction. The programme material can be reproduced on a format of any quality, and may not be in stereo.

Low quality formats

Low-quality formats include:

1. Optical sound 16 mm formats.
2. Video cassette recorders (not hi-fi).
3. Standard U-matic industrial formats.

High quality formats

High-quality formats include:

1. Video cassettes with hi-fi sound systems.
2. Video discs.
3. Television transmission, using digital sound.

Between these two quality extremes are:

1. 35 mm optical soundtracks with noise reduction.
2. Analogue sound television transmissions systems.
3. 35 mm and 70 mm striped magnetic picture prints.

In the cinema the sound reproducing chain from final mix to released motion picture film is comparatively short. In television transmissions the chain is much longer.

The television chain

Replayed from the telecine machine or videotape recorder, audio post-produced sound and pictures for broadcasting are routed to the transmission area of the television station where they are monitored, equalized and then fed to their correct destination. This area also routes tie lines, intercoms, control signals, and provides all the necessary equipment needed to generate pulses for scanning, coding, and synchronizing video throughout the station.

Sound in stereo form is usually sent in a simple left/right format. The problems of routing stereo signals are very much greater than routing mono; not only must the signals maintain the same level left and right, but they must also maintain phase.

Although it is possible to route stereo signals using matrix systems (e.g. M & S), discrete channels are usually used so as to reduce complications in mixing and processing of the signal. Matrixed signals are useful in transmission broadcasting but complicated to distribute and record. Monitoring the signal can create problems, since it needs to be returned to its discrete format to be audible. In addition, matrix signals suffer loss of stereo separation rather more easily than discrete left and right signals.

Any television organization using stereo must produce a db attenuation standard for the mono sum programme signals (produced from the left plus right stereo signals), and this figure must be standardized throughout the transmitting network. Stereo signals are usually monitored on left and right meters, with an additional third meter used to indicate the mono signals. More useful than a meter is the XY oscilloscope, which will show any instant out-of-phase condition. These are particularly important if the transmitting chain is long and complicated. In America, for example, a large network broadcasting company may have two network distribution centres, one on the east coast, and one on the west coast, each distributing sound and pictures over satellite and terrestrial systems. These network centres can integrate programmes from, videotape, film, remote pick-ups (outside broadcasts), and live studios. There are many pieces of equipment in the chain which include satellites, studio and transmitter links, processing devices, transformers, equalizers and much more. When the links are joined together, the effects of their individual degradations are cumulative and without proper metering or monitoring, the task of discovering the source of a problem can be enormous.

Further problems are created when a video delay line is introduced into the video picture. This eliminates the possibility of frame roll as a video signal is switched from one video source to another using a different sync pulse train. The incoming video signal is delayed so that the sync pulses are coincident. In PAL this difference of timing is 40 milliseconds and in NTSC television systems 33 milliseconds, thus a difference between the audio and video synchronization is created (similar problems exist when pictures are sent by satellite and sound by landlines). This delay is unfortunately 'the wrong way round'; in our natural environment we are used to receiving an audible stimulus slightly after a visual stimulus. Sound travels much slower than light, and it has been measured that over speaking distances, the visual sensation of seeing the lips move, arrives at the brain about 18 milliseconds before the aural sensation. To our brains this has become a natural order but television has turned this upside down. To restore this lip sync, audio delay lines are used.

In American the National Association of Broadcasters (NAB), has specified that audio to visual synchronization must be kept to less than 25 milliseconds for advance and 40 milliseconds in delay. If programme material has varying synchronization it is far better to keep the audio behind the picture than ahead of it, and also to go into synchronization at the end of a faulty section, rather than to start in synchronization and then go out of synchronization.

In transmission, a video signal leaves the studio centre by a microwave link or a co-axial line. The accompanied sound may be carried on a high-quality audio line, or in the video signal using a pulse code modulation technique, which inserts the audio into the line synchronizing pulses (sound in syncs). This has three major advantages:

1. The quality is better since it is digital.
2. It does not require a separate sound circuit and is therefore cheaper.
3. There is no possibility of the wrong picture source going with the wrong sound source.

Transmission of television signals

Television signals can be transmitted into the home through cables, through the atmosphere from earthbound transmitters, or through space, from satellites.

The signals transmitted through the atmosphere or space are essentially radiated frequencies vibrating above the frequency of the audio spectrum. It is only when current alternates at these so called radio frequencies, of 20 kHz to 13 Mcs and beyond, that energy is thrown off and in such a way as to radiate and be received over distances.

These radio waves, like the signal generated around a wire carrying audio, are both electrical and magnetic. Their frequency distinguishes one from another. In a radio wave the electric and magnetic fields are at right angles to each other and to the direction of propagation. They are said to be horizontally polarized if the electric field varies in strength from side to side, and the magnetic field varies in strength from top to bottom. Vertical polarization is the reverse of this and usually denoted by the letter 'V', whereas horizontal polarization is denoted by the letter 'H'. This polarization can be seen in terrestrial television aerials, which have either horizontal or vertical rods clearly indicating the type of polarization used. Satellite dishes must be arranged accordingly. However, transmissions from direct broadcasting satellites (DBS), are not only polarized vertically and horizontally, but also in a circular manner. This can be either left-hand or right-hand, LHC and RHC (left and right-hand circular).

The speed of any radio wave is always the same whatever its frequency. Denoted by the letter 'C', it is equal to 186 000 miles per second, that is the speed of light, which is the fastest speed known in the universe. Despite this speed, pictures bounced off the moon take over a second to arrive at the earth and even by live satellite, programme material takes over a quarter of a second to arrive.

The length in space of one cycle (or one vibration) is called the wavelength, and is measured in metres. This wavelength is spread over 'C' metres; therefore a radio station broadcasting on a frequency of 600 khz has a wave length, of the speed of the frequency of a radio wave in space, (C) divided by its own frequency, which equals 500 metres.

It is now necessary to modulate the audio signals onto this radio frequency carrier wave. For television transmission the video signals are frequency modulated on the carrier, in a similar manner to the way video signals are recorded. The sound is transmitted on a slightly different frequency to that of the vision, allowing sound and vision to be processed separately.

In the UK system the total channel width of the television signal is 8 MHz, the vision width is 5.5 MHz and the sound vision separation 6 MHz. Audio signals up to 15 khz can be transmitted using analogue techniques.

Stereo television sound

Stereo sound for television can be transmitted in various ways, but the main concerns of any system must be to ensure that the stereo sound does not affect the quality of the mono transmission, and that the transmitted area in stereo is the same as for mono.

For compatibility with an existing system the main channel carries the sum signal, the 'M' (L + R) which is mono, and a sub-carrier usually carries the additional difference signal, the 'S', which when matrixed with the 'M' signal, produces stereo sound.

In America, a system similar to FM stereo radio transmission is used. Originally designed by Zenith and General Electric in the 1950s, it includes compansion. The 'S' signal is modulated onto a separate sub-carrier, and a third pilot signal is also radiated that ensures the receiver circuits lock correctly in order to produce stereo. There is also a third sound channel available (Secondary Audio Programme, SAP), which can be broadcast and decoded separately from the main and stereo channels – making mono bilingual programming possible. The system is capable of transmitting a signal extending to 15 khz. Although successful in the USA, and with excellent compatibility, it can suffer from buzz-on-sound interference from vision – particularly in European broadcasting transmission systems. In Japan and West Germany, two FM carriers are used to transmit stereo. In Britain, an entirely separate digital system is used.

Unfortunately, digital 'sound in syncs' systems cannot be successfully transmitted and received domestically since the pictures may well suffer from dancing dots appearing on the screen. Digital transmission is possible, however, by the use of an additional stereo signal, pulse code modulated onto a second carrier. In Britain this is spaced 6.552 MHz above the vision, and digitally modulated at a rate of 7.28 K bits/second. The resolution is achieved by using compansion to 14 bits/second although it is transmitted at only 10 bits/second. It is called 'Nicam', (Near Instantaneous Companded), and gives the highest sound quality of any television transmission system. The format is similar to that of the MAC (Multiplexed Analogue Components) systems which have been agreed for use in European Direct Broadcast satellite transmissions.

Satellites

Satellites receive their signals from ground stations via microwave links. Arriving at the satellite, the signal is converted to the satellite's transmitting frequency and then sent back down to earth. In the European DBS system, the transmitting frequencies are in the range of 11.7 to 12.5 GHz the carrier having a band width of 27 MHz, which is much higher than any terrestrial television system.

Any transmitted wave, from whatever source, has to contend with both absorption from the ground or the atmosphere, and reflection. Waves of low frequency are readily absorbed by the earth and objects in their path, and since losses increase with frequency, ground wave transmission is unsatisfactory over any long distances.

Higher frequencies are, therefore, used in broadcasting, which take advantage of the ionosphere, (layers of ionized air between 100 and 1000 kilometres above the earth). These layers can be used to bounce radio waves back to earth, like a radio mirror. However, these reflections back to earth begin to fail at radio frequencies of about 100 MHz, and completely disappear at about 2 gigahertz (GHz). At this point the waves travel straight through the ionosphere. The ionosphere is of no use whatsoever for mirroring back terrestrial television signals, the lowest of which is in the ultra-high frequency range. Terrestrial television is therefore radiated over short distances, with many transmitting stations making up for the ground losses.

Satellites transmit at even higher frequencies than terrestrial television systems. They can project straight through the ionosphere with little interference, (in the space above the ionosphere there are no transmitting losses) so transmission can be over very long distances. This means that one satellite can cover an area that would normally require several hundred terrestrial transmitters.

Whereas over 600 stations might be necessary to cover Britain using earth-bound terrestrial television transmissions, one satellite can do the same job, with its foot print covering much of Europe as well, although, there are obviously language problems and cultural barriers to overcome.

Domestic video cassette machines

Television programmes and films do not necessarily have to be transmitted to be viewed in the home. They can be distributed by video cassettes, and although not in the original recording format they are often in the final format for video and film viewing.

All domestic video formats provide stereo sound facilities. Originally, the audio track on the domestic video recorder was of very poor quality because of the narrow tracks and the very slow speeds. However, audio frequency modulation recording is now available on these formats, producing good quality hi-fi sound.

Despite these vast improvements in video cassette sound quality, most consumers still listen on the linear tracks of non hi-fi recorders. Those involved in audio post production should be aware of the inadequacies of video cassette sound and the vast differences in sound quality between hi-fi and 'normal' formats.

The VHS format

This was announced by JVC in 1976 and now holds the lead over its only serious competitor, the Beta format. The video recording system is similar to that used in the professional U-matic system. The VHS format uses two audio tracks of 0.35 mm in width each with a guard band of 0.3 mm. There is no guard band between the audio track and the tape edge; this makes the format susceptible to problems of poor tape splitting. Recording pre-emphasis and de-emphasis is employed at a tape speed of 1.313 inches per second (3.3 cm/sec). Dolby 'B' noise reduction is available on many machines. On the standard analogue tracks, an audio band width up to 10 kHz is possible.

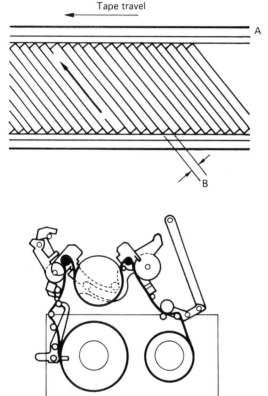

VHS tracks, tape width 12.65 mm; A, Audio track 1.00 mm; B, Video track 0.049 mm; C, Lacing pattern (*Courtesy of Sony Broadcast & Communications*)

Beta format

Introduced by the Sony Corporation, Beta was first demonstrated in 1975. Three versions of the format have been produced. Only Beta II and III are now available. The sound is recorded longitudinally, running at a speed of 0.79 inches per second (2.0 cm/sec) and the two tracks are 1.05 mm in width. Frequencies up to 7 K can be recorded on the standard analogue tracks.

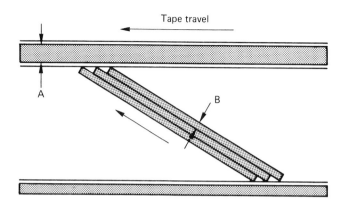

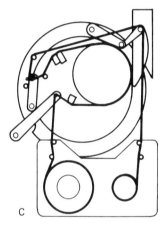

Betamax tracks, tape width 12.65 mm; A, Audio track 1.05 mm; B, Video track 0.0328 mm; C, Lacing pattern (*Courtesy of Sony Broadcast & Communications*)

Beta Hi-Fi

The poor sound quality of the Beta format encouraged Sony to produce an improved Beta system. This was called Beta Hi-Fi. In the hi-fi format, audio frequency modulation recording is used with a noise reduction system, and low and high frequency pre-emphasis. The manufacturers claim an 80 db signal to noise ratio, with harmonic distortion less than 1% below clipping. Band widths extend to 20 kHz. This system is peculiar to America, for in Europe the PAL standard video recording spectrum does not have sufficient room for the insertion of the hi-fi carrier into the picture recording system, and a VHS Hi-Fi type audio system is used.

VHS Hi-Fi

VHS followed quickly on the Beta Hi-Fi system with their own format. The VHS system modulates the tape using separate heads to those used in the video system, a compression and expansion system, and pre-emphasis and audio FM modulation. The audio is recorded below the video using a system called Depth Multiplex recording. Audio is first recorded on the tape from heads on the video drum. Video signals are then recorded over this, but only at the surface of the tape. It is possible for these two signals be decoded separately later, in replay. VHS Hi-Fi is of similar quality to the Beta Hi-Fi format. Analogue tracks are also provided to create compatibility with standard VHS tapes.

Super VHS

Super VHS was launched in the USA in 1987 and Europe in 1988. It produces compatible pictures of a quality superior to standard VHS. The sound is recorded in a similar way to VHS Hi-Fi.

Video hi-fi formats are particularly sensitive to poor alignment. If the mechanical adjustments are imperfect there will be poor head switching and interruptions in the video signal. As a result, the audio will contain a low buzzing noise. This in turn creates problems in decoding the compression and expansion systems, particularly, on low level signals where the buzzing can even modulate the track.

The various standards that exist even within one format are even more of a problem. Minor variations can be found in the pre-emphasis used by different manufacturers and even by the same manufacturer.

Domestic pulse code modulation recording – video 8

The video 8 format is designed to record PCM signals with video, and thus offers an alternative to an audio FM recording. The 10 bit digital signal is reduced to 8 bits. This signal is read continuously into a memory and read out at seven times speeds. The effective head wrap is between 180 and 220 degrees, and the first 30 degrees of the wrap are used to record the PCM signals. The signal is companded and FM modulated. The audio signal, although an 8 bit quantization signal, is equivalent to a 14 bit system through special processing. An upgraded version of video 8 is also available and it is of similar video quality to SVHS.

Optical video discs

The optical video disc was first introduced in Europe in 1977. It is used mainly to play back motion picture films in the home. Picture quality is superior to that of the standard video cassette recorder and its sound quality is similar to any digital recording system. Since there is no contact on playback between the disc and the pick-up laser, the discs have an unlimited life. They are most popular in Japan, where the video cassette recorder has not gained the acceptance it has in Europe and America.

The discs are recorded and manufactured in a similar way to compact discs and the information is replayed by a laser beam pick-up device. Audio is available as an FM signal or as a PCM signal.

Surround sound

Dolby Surround is the consumer side of Dolby Stereo. It is a two track matrixed system. Dolby material can be issued on stereo video discs and video cassettes. These programmes are compatible for surround sound decoders used in the home.

Glossary

Access time   The time taken to retrieve video or sound information from a store, which might be in the form of a video or audio tape recorder, a sound-effects library etc.

Address   A time or location within programme material; often selected as a 'go to' for machines via time code.

AFM   Audio frequency modulation. See *Frequency modulation*.

Ambience   See *Presence*.

Amplitude   The maximum height of a wave form at any given point.

Analogue (audio and video)   A signal which is a direct physical representation of the wave form, in, for example – voltage, magnetism or optical modulation.

ANSI   American National Standards Institute.

Assembly   The first process of editing, usually applied to film, when the various shots are joined together in a rough order to produce a rough cut. In video to edit further means additional copying that may be unacceptable from a quality point of view.

Assembly editing   Video editing by adding one shot after another each shot using its own control track. Therefore a picture roll may take place at the edit. See *Insert editing*.

Attenuate   To reduce the amplitude or intensity of a sound.

Auto assembly/conforming   The assembling of an edited master from a previous edit decision list (EDL) using a computerized edit controller.

Back time   The calculation of a start point by first finding the finish point and subtracting the duration. This can relate to edit points or the recording of narration.

Balanced line   A method of sending a signal via two wires, neither of which are directly tied to the earth of the system. If an external electrical field is induced into the circuit leads, it is in phase in both leads simultaneously. This unwanted signal will be eliminated by cancellation at the balanced input point, while the alternating audio signal passes through, unaffected.

Bel   A relative measure of sound intensity or volume. It expresses the ratio of one sound to another and is calculated as a logarithm. (A decibel is a tenth of a Bel).

Betacam (SP)   A Sony trademark, a professional half-inch inch video format with resolution approaching that of one inch C format. SP means superior performance.

Bias   A high frequency alternating current (up to 120 kHz) fed into an analogue magnetic recording circuit to assist the recording process.

Black burst   Blacking; colour black; edit black. Provides synchronizing signals for a system to lock onto for stabilizing a videotape recorder.

Blanking level   The zero signal level in a video signal. Below this is sync information, above this visible picture.

Blimp   A soundproof cover to reduce the mechanical noise from a film camera.

Bloop   An opaque patch painted over an optical soundtrack join to eliminate a click on reproduction.

Bouncing   Recording, mixing, replaying and then recording again within the audio tracks of an audio or videotape recorder.

Burnt in time code (window dub, USA)   Time code transferred with picture from the time code track of a videotape and visually displayed in the picture as part of the image. This can only be used on copies for audio post-production use. The burnt in time code is accurate in still frame, whereas the time code figure from the longitudinal coded track is invariably wrong.

C format   A one inch tape, reel to reel, video recording format of high quality, using analogue recording techniques developed by Sony and Ampex.

Camcorder   A combined video camera and recorder, usually in broadcast form in Beta or M format. Often similar in size and facilities to a film camera.

Capacitance   A measurement of the electrical storing ability of a capacitor or condenser measured in farads.

Cathode ray tube (CRT)   The picture tube of a television monitor, visual display unit, or phase meter.

Clapper board, clap sticks   A pair of hinged boards which are banged together at the beginning of a film double system sound shoot, to help synchronize sound and picture if time code is not used. The clapper usually has an identification board as well.

Clash   The term used to describe the point at which the two ribbons of a light valve come into contact and produce heavy distortion.

Clean FX   Effects which have no additional unwanted sounds.

Click track   A sound with a regular beat used for timing in music scoring – now produced electronically, but once made by punching holes at regular intervals in film and reproducing this through an optical sound head.

Colour framing   In PAL the sequence of 8 fields (4 frames) which comprises the repetition rate of the matching set of fields. (NTSC 4 fields: 2 frames) with videotape composite recording (one-inch or 2 inch). The tape is only correctly edited if field 8 is followed by field 1. If this does not take place, a flash or jump will accompany the edit.

Combined print   A positive film on which picture and sound have been both printed.

Compression   A method of reducing the volume range of sound.

Console (desk)   Colloquial term for an audio mixing device, called a 'desk' in Britain.

Control track   A regular pulse that is generated during videotape recording for synchronizing, it provides a reference for tracking control and tape speed and is found at the edge of the tape.

CPU   Central processing unit, the main brain of a computer.

Crash   A systems failure in a computer.

Crosstalk   In stereo equipment a crosstalk occurs when some of the left-hand signal leaks into the right-hand signal, and *vice-versa*. Time code signals can also crosstalk into adjacent audio tracks. It can also apply to electrical interference of any kind.

Crystal lock   A system of driving a video or audio tape recorder at a known speed, at high accuracy, usually better than within one frame in ten minutes. The timing/synchronizing signal is derived from an oscillating quartz crystal.

Cut away   A shot other than the main action added to a scene, often used to avoid a jump cut or to bridge time.

Dailies   See *Rushes*.

db decibel   A convenient logarithmic measure for voltage ratios and sound levels. One tenth of a Bel, a 1 db change is a very small but perceptible change in loudness. A three db change is equal to double the power of the signal. A six db change is the equivalent to doubling the perceived loudness.

De-esser   A device for reducing sibilant distortion.

Desk   See *Console*.

D format   D1 and D2 digital video recording formats.

Digital (audio and video)   A signal where the waveform is encoded into binary form for storage or processing. This signal can be copied repeatedly without degradation (compare with analogue).

Discontinuous shooting   Shooting video or film with one camera and moving the camera position for each change of shot.

Distortion   An unwanted change in a signal – the difference between the original sound and that reproduced by the recording machine. Distortion takes many forms, frequency, phase or non-linear. Non-linear distortion is usually measured as harmonic or intermodulation distortion and has an 'edgy' sound. Digital recording offers the maximum potential for distortion free recording.

Double system recording   Double system or separate sound recording. This is a production method which employs separate machinery to record sound and picture – it is used in film sound recording.

Drop frame   American system of time code generation which adjusts the generated data every minute to compensate for the speed of the NTSC television system running at 29.97 frames per second.

Drop out   A momentary reduction or loss of signal, usually used with reference to tape or magnetic film.

Edited master   The final edited videotape with continuous programme material and time code.

Edit points, edit in, edit out   The beginning and end points of an edit when a video programme is being assembled or soundtrack being recorded.

Effects   Sound effects, FX for short.

Equalization (eq.)   The boosting or decreasing of the intensity of low, middle or high frequencies to change the 'sound' of programme material. Equalization is also used in tape machines to overcome losses in the recording processes. Equalization characteristics are recommended in the USA by the NAB and in Europe by the IEC.

Event number   A number assigned by an editor to each edit in an edit decision list.

Exciter lamp   The lamp in an optical sound reproducing machine whose light is focused onto a photo-electric cell. It is the interruption of this light by the varying density of the film that causes variations of the output of the cell and this amplified produces sound.

Foley (USA only)   Creating sound effects by watching picture and duplicating the actions. Post-syncing effects in GB.

Frame   One film picture, one complete video scanning cycle.

Free run   Applied in time code to the recording of time code from a generator that runs continuously. A recording therefore has discontinuous time code at each stop and start. See also *record run*.

Freeze frame   The showing of one single frame of a videotape or film. See also '*still in the gate*'.

Frequency   The number of times of an occurrence in a given time, e.g. frequency per second, in sound (called Hertz). (See chart opposite.)

Frequency modulation   A method of encoding a signal whereby the programme material varies the frequency of a carrier signal – the level of the carrier remaining constant. Audio examples include stereo VHF radio and the hi-fi tracks of some domestic video cassette recorders and in the Betacam and M broadcast formats. AFM recording gives excellent signal to noise ratio and frequency response. In video recorders it is recorded within the spinning head drum resulting in low 'wow' and 'flutter', which contributes to the good dynamic range.

Full coat/stripe (fully coated GB)   Full(y) coat(ed) film stock has oxide across the entire width of the film. Stripe has the oxide just in the area where the recording takes place – this allows the transparent material to be written upon.

FX   Short for sound effects.

Gain   The extent to which an amplifier is able to increase the amplitude of a given signal; the ratio of input to the output level.

Gamma   The degree of contrast attained in a photographic image. In optical recording it needs to be at a maximum.

Gen lock   A system whereby all video equipment is locked to a common video synchronizing generator allowing all to be synchronized together for editing etc. It is vital that time code is also in synchronization with the video if computer controlled editing is to be used.

Guide track   A soundtrack made or reproduced to help post-synchronization, and not intended to be part of the final mix.

Haas effect   A psychoacoustic phenomenon where the mind identifies the first place from which a sound is heard as the origin of the sound, ignoring other sources of sound arriving a fraction of a second later. (Used in Dolby Stereo).

Hard lock   Synchronization accuracy to part of a frame, producing accurate picture edits but possibly increasing 'wow' and 'flutter' on sound.

Hardware   The physical components that form part of an audio post-production system – for example, the tape recorders, video player, and computer.

Header (USA)   A leader at the beginning of a programme.

Head out   Tape is stored on the reel with the programme material head out – recommended for videotape storage, rather than audio tape.

Hexadecimal display   A facility for displaying sixteen discrete characters 0–9 and A–F, as found in a time code display.

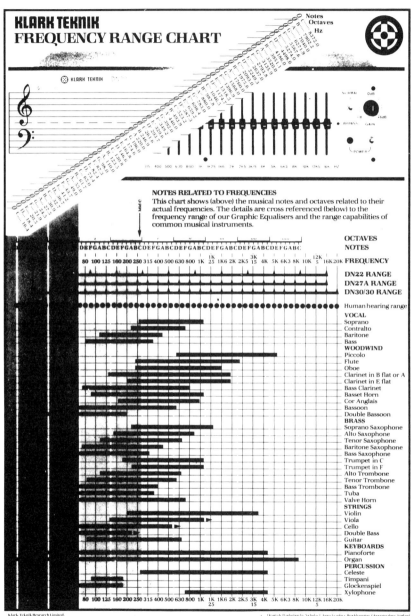

Frequency Range Chart

Frequency range chart (*Courtesy of Klark-Teknik Research Ltd*)

Hi-fi (high fidelity)   A term coined for the consumer market to describe state of the art audio quality and equipment.

Hunting   Movements backwards and forwards across a selected synchronous locating point, caused by poor line-up of equipment.

IEC   International Electronic Committee, a European Standards body.

Impedance   The opposition to the passage of electric current by the resistance and reactance of a circuit. In a tape head wound with many coils of fine wire, there is a high impedance. A low impedance head is wound with fewer turns of thicker wire.

Inductance   A device which provides a magnetic opposition to any growth or decay of electrical current – such as a choke or coil.

'In point'   The beginning of an edit, the first frame to be recorded.

Insert editing   Editing where control track, time code, and black level have been already recorded on the tape (pre striped); video picture material is added as the edit progresses (as opposed to assembly editing).

Intelligent synchronizer   A micro computer that monitors machines in audio post-production situations and learns their ballists and operational characteristics in order to speed up synchronization.

Interlock   A term to indicate that two or more pieces of equipment are running in synchronization.

Intermodulation   The result of the interaction of two or more frequencies – the amplitude of one is modulated at the frequency of another.

Jam sync   A process of locking a time code generator to an existing coded tape so as to extend or replace the code. Used when code is of poor quality.

Jog   A function on a video or audio tape recorder which allows tape to be moved at any speed through stop to single speed with pictures forward and reverse. (See *Shuttle*.)

Jump cut   A cut which breaks continuity.

Kinescope recording (GB telerecording)   A film made off a television screen.

Laying sound   To place sound in its desired relationship to picture.

Leader   In America identified as a leader or trail leader. The leader gives a countdown to programme start. In film using flashing numbers, in video a clock. See *Run-up/run-out*.

Level   Volume of a sound. See also *VU meter*. *Peak programme meter*.

Level cut, straight cut (Editorial cut, USA)   A point where sound and picture cut at the same point.

Level synchronization   A point where picture and soundtracks are in alignment. USA term, editorial sync.

Longitudinal time code (LTC)   Time code information recorded as an audio signal on a VTR or audio tape recorder.

Loop   A loop of material running sound continuously. It may be an NAB cartridge, a digital sampler, or a piece of sprocketed film. The term looping refers to post-synchronization.

M & E   A music and effects soundtrack, that includes information that is only relevant to international sales, i.e. there is no dialogue.

MII format   A trademark of Matsushita/Panasonic. A professional half-inch video cassette format with a quality approaching one inch C format.

Mag track   Sprocketed magnetic film.

Married print   Synonymous with a combined print in film.

Master   An original recording, video or audio, e.g. master edit, master magnetic (film sound), master multitrack, master music etc.

Matching   Equalizing sounds so that they appear similar, for example, dialogue in discontinuous shooting.

Microsecond (ms)   One millionth of a second.

MIL   Longitudinal measure equal to one thousandth of an inch.

Millisecond (ms)   One thousandth of a second.

Mix   In sound, the combining of sounds. In vision, a dissolve.

Mixing console/desk   See *Console*.

Modulate   To vary from a mean position.

Movieola   Trade name for a film editing machine, an upright model usually favoured in the USA.

MTS   Multichannel television sound. An American system of stereo audio compatible with the NTSC system. It consists of a pair of 15 k bandwidth channels, a separate audio programme channel (SAP) and a narrow bandwidth professional usage channel.

Multi camera shooting   Using many cameras to cover a scene, all shooting at the same time; opposite of discontinuous shooting.

Multitrack recorder   An audio recorder with multiple recording tracks using one tape.

NAB   National Association of Broadcasters. (An American organization.)

NC   Noise contour. A set of criteria used to assess the quietness of a room.

Nearfield monitors   Speakers used in close proximity to the sound engineer.

Neopilot   A synchronizing pulsed tape system developed by Kodelski.

Noise reduction (NR)   A method of reducing the inherent background noise in a recording or transmission system. Available types include: Dolby SR; Dolby A; Dolby B; Dolby C.

NTSC   National Television Standards Committee. The initials NTSC usually refer to the colour television system primarily used in the USA and Japan, based on a 60 hz mains system using 525 lines.

Octave   A musical interval spanning eight full notes. This is a 2:1 span of frequencies. Human hearing spans ten octaves.

Off-line edit   The editing of material using low cost equipment – for later assembly, on-line with high-quality equipment.

Offset   The positioning, usually of a tape recorder, away from its normal synchronized position. The machines run continually with the offset in position. Offset is measured in time and frames.

On-line video edit   Editing from information produced using an off-line video edit suite. This may be manual from notes, semi-automatic, or automatic from a floppy computer disc.

On-the-fly   Working while the system is on the move. Choosing events points or edit points, or mixing without stopping.

Oscillator   A device for producing pure-tone electric waves which are frequency-calibrated.

Overshoot   To modulate a recording beyond its recommended level and thus introduce distortion.

Pad   A fixed attenuator.

Parallel data   In time code, time code in binary coded decimal form suitable for data output to an external unit. c.f. serial data.

Patch   To make a temporary connection between fixed cable terminals at a (patch) by using a short length of cable called a patch cord.

Peak programme meter (IEC)   An audio meter with a characteristic defined by the IEC.

Phase difference   The time delay between two time varying waves expressed as an angle.

Phase scope   A form of oscilloscope having the ability to show phase relations between audio signals.

Ping ponging   See *Bouncing*.

Pink noise   Random noise with a frequency spectrum that appears to be equal at all frequencies to the human ear. Its random nature makes it representative of actual programme conditions. It can be generated by filtering white noise with a filter that has a slope of 3 db/octave.

Polarity   Positive or negative direction. The way of connecting a pair of signal conductors – in phase or reverse phase.

Pre-roll   The time allowed before the start of a programme or edit to allow the equipment, video or audio, to come up to speed and synchronize (usually between 3 and 10 seconds).

Presence   The natural background sound that a location possesses without dialogue or other spot sounds. Presence is used to fill 'holes' created during editing. Also called room time, ambience or fill.

Printing   A term used in film for copying or dubbing off picture or sound, e.g. printing a soundtrack, copying it.

Print through   Transfer of one magnetic field from one layer of recording tape or film to the next on the reel. Pre-echo on tapes stored head out, post echo on tapes stored tail out.

Pulsed tape   An audio tape with a speed reference signal in the form of a pulse. A pulsed mono quarter-inch tape has 60 hz (USA) or 50 hz (Europe) recorded on it. This signal is used to dub the tape onto sprocketed film in synchronization.

Punching in/out   The selection of record on a video or audio system, usually on-the-fly.

Rank cintel   A telecine machine for transferring film to videotape, usually with colour correction ability.

Real time   Actual elapsed time.

Record run   Applied in time code to the practice of running code only when the recorder, video or audio, is in record mode. The code is therefore sequential on the tape despite the machine being switched on and off over a period of time. See *Free run*.

Re-framing   Reconstituting time code where the time code waveform is mistimed relative to the video waveform. A de-coder cannot therefore determine which video frame the time code word refers to. Se also *Gen. lock.*

Restored code   Replayed time code processed to improve its quality.

Reverberation   The persistence of sound in an enclosed space due to reflections from the enclosing surfaces.

RMS   Root mean square: a method of measuring level where the true power of the signal is calculated. Short spikes or peaks in the signal have only a small effect on long-term readings. The signal is squared, the average taken and the square root taken.

Run-up/run-out (USA)   The blank tape or film used for threading at the beginning and end of a recording. No test signals or programme material should be recorded on it. (In Britain, called leader.)

Rushes   The first viewing of camera and sound material after it has been returned from film processing, or has been recorded.

Safety copy   A copy of a master to be used if the master is damaged.

Scoring   The recording of music for a programme or motion picture after it has been edited.

Separate sound recording   See *Double system recording.*

Serial data   In time code, code with all 80 or 90 bits in correct sequence, i.e. data in a continuous stream from one source.

Servo   An electronic circuit which, for example, controls the capstan speed of a recorder. The servo may be adjusted by an external source for audio post-production synchronizers.

Shoot to 'playback'   Playback of a soundtrack on location so that action may be synchronized to it.

Shuttle   Variable running of a video or tape recorder up to high speed from single speed.

Signal to noise ratio – S/N   This can be considered as follows:
1. The difference in db between maximum permissible signal level and the noise that is present while the maximum signal is present.
2. The difference in db between the maximum permissible signal level and the residual noise.
3. The difference in db between a given signal level and the residual noise.

Silent drop in (punch in)   When actuating the record button, a silent drop in is achieved without any extraneous sound being recorded.

Slate   An announcement, visual or aural, that gives identifying information for a recording.

SMPTE   The Society of Motion Picture and Television Engineers.

Soft lock   Synchronization to an accuracy of plus or minus one frame, used to reduce the possibilities of wow and flutter in audio followers.

Software   A computer term for the instructions loaded into a computer for directing its operation.

Spacing   Blank film stock used to separate one sound from another in a soundtrack. In USA called leader.

SPL   Sound pressure level. The measure of the loudness of an acoustic sound expressed in db. 0 db SPL is near the threshold of hearing. 120+ db is near the threshold of pain.

Split edit   An edit where the sound and vision start or finish at different times.

Spot effects   Spot sounds that are not continuous and go with a specific action.

Sprocket   The driving wheel or synchronizing wheel of a film apparatus provided with teeth to engage the perforations of the film.

Standard conversion   The converting of television pictures from one format to another, e.g. NTSC 525 lines 60 hz to PAL 625 lines 50 hz.

Striping   Pre-recording a tape with time code or a video signal, so allowing it to be used in post-production.

Tail out (Tails out USA)   Tape wound so that rewinding is necessary prior to playing – often recommended for audio tape storage.

Tape speed   The speed at which magnetic recording tape passes the recording heads in inches per second, e.g. 30 ips, 15 ips, 7½ ips are used in professional recording.

Telerecording (kinescope recording, USA)   A film made from photographing a television screen.

Thin   Colloquial term applied to sound lacking in lower frequencies.

Three stripe (USA)   See *Triple track.*

Time compression   A technique where the play speed of a recording is increased above the recorded speed. A pitch change device lowers the resultant pitch back to normal, resulting in a shorter actual time but correct sound quality.

Transient response   The response of an amplifier or recording device to a very short fast-rising signal. A measurement of the quality of a recording system.

Trim   To add or subtract time from or 'trim' an edit.

Triple track   35 mm sprocketed magnetic film with three distinct soundtracks; dialogue, music and sound effects. Known as three stripe in USA.

U-matic   A standard three-quarter inch video cassette format, used in industrial and broadcast applications.

Upcut (USA)   The loss of the beginning of an audio source, caused when an edit point is late, e.g. the loss of the first syllable of dialogue in a sentence.

User bits   Undefined bits in the 80 bit EBU/SMPTE time code word. Available for uses other than time information.

Variable area soundtrack   A system of recording sound on film in which the track is divided into two areas; one clear, one black. Used in Dolby Stereo optical recording.

Variable density soundtrack   A system of recording sound on film now obsolete in which the track is of uniform density across its width but in which the density varies as the film moves.

VCR (video cassette recorder)   Enclosed video tape in three-quarter inch U-matic. VHS or Beta form are half-inch.

Vertical internal time code (VITC)   Time code for video – encoded into the video signal, it can be replayed when the tape is stationary since the video-head is rotating – an advantage in finding cues in audio post-production. However, VITC cannot be easily decoded at high speed since videotape recorders suffer from picture break-up in this mode.

Voice over   Explanatory speech, non-synchronous, superimposed over sound effects and music. Also called commentary or narration.

VU meter   A volume units meter that measures the average volume of sound signals in decibels and is intended to to indicate the perceived loudness of a signal.

Wavelength   The distance between the crests of a wave form.

White noise   Random noise with an even distribution of frequencies within the audio spectrum. This form of noise occurs naturally in transistors and resistors.

Wild track   A soundtrack which has been recorded separately from the picture, wild, without synchronizing.

Wow   Slow variations in speed of a reproduced sound from the mean due to inaccuracies in the mechanics of the system, expressed as a percentage.

Index

Page references to illustrations are given in italics.